GAMES ON THE GO

SANDY BERAM

Collier Books

A Division of Macmillan Publishing Co., Inc.

NEW YORK

Collier Macmillan Publishers

LONDON

*To my father, who taught me my first
car game, and to Harvey and the
children, who make my whole life a
wonderful game—both in and out of
the car*

Library of Congress Catalog Card Number 79-12412

Macmillan Publishing Co., Inc.
866 Third Avenue, New York, N.Y. 10022
Collier Macmillan Canada, Ltd.

Library of Congress Cataloging in Publication Data
Beram, Sandy.
    Games on the go.
    SUMMARY: Suggests more than 160 games and variations
that can be played while traveling.
    1. Travel.   [1. Games for travelers]
I. Title.
GV1206.B47   793   79-12412
ISBN 0-02-048570-0 (lib. ed.)
ISBN 0-02-028150-1 (with coupons)

First Printing 1979

Printed in the United States of America

Contents

Introduction

"Are we almost there?"

To most parents this is the refrain of any trip, repeated regularly from start to finish. Bored and restless, children can't wait to get "there." With the games in this book, however, you can make traveling with your children almost as pleasant and carefree as traveling without them. Instead of complaining every few minutes, your children may well groan with disappointment when you arrive at your destination.

On the pages which follow, you will find over 150 easy-to-play games and variations which I compiled, adapted, and, in most cases, invented to avoid boredom and pandemonium in my own car. Nearly two dozen of them can be played aloud and require no equipment. At least 95 require nothing more than a felt pen, paper, and a watch or egg timer.

The games range from peaceful pastimes such as Night Lights or Triangle Treasure Hunt to exciting contests like Highway Baseball or the Waving Game. There are board games to delight game-lovers of all ages, card games for the card sharks, challenging brain-teasers, and a variety of absorbing highway observation games. Most have adaptations for one player and need no adult supervision. Many can be played by children as young as three or four.

Every game lists a suggested age range, the length of time you will need, and the necessary materials and preparation, most of which can be done in the car. For your convenience, each chapter ends with a complete list of materials you'll need to play any game in that chapter. There are tips to help your road party run as smoothly as possible and even a few physical games to help the kids work off excess energy in a closed space.

So the next time you're ready to hit the road—whether for a cross-country trip or a hop across your city—don't forget to bring along *Games on the Go*. It's sure to supply you with countless ways to get more happy miles per gallon!

Sandy Beram

TIPS
1·TFT
FOR TRIPS

It's tempting to skip over a chapter on helpful hints and jump right into a book—in this case, the games themselves. However, this chapter will help you avoid some of the pitfalls my family has learned from experience and will help you enjoy all the games you play.

Eager participants are always the most important ingredient for a successful game. There are some days when my family is in just the right frame of mind to enjoy the challenge of car games. But there are lazy days, too, when the only thing we feel like doing is resting or having a quiet conversation. While I certainly encourage you to plan some games and activities to enjoy on the road, use your own judgment about when to use them. Forced fun won't make anyone happy. When my family travels, I usually plan two types of games—some that the kids can play without adult guidance and some that we can all enjoy together. I also bring along one or two quiet things that the kids can do alone.

Here are some tips to help you get organized:

Safety first The most important factor to consider in a car is safety, and this goes for games, too.

The driver should never participate in a game which requires him to take his eyes off the road, even when he or she is the only person in the car with a child. If there are two adults in the car and both drive, they may decide to take turns at the wheel so that each can get a chance to enjoy a game with the children while taking a break from driving.

If a game requires writing, it's better to use a crayon or felt-tip pen rather than a pencil. If the car stops short, any sharp, pointed object is a potential hazard.

When children are playing highway observation games, remind them never to stick their heads or arms out of the window and always be sure that the doors are locked.

Getting ready For most of these games, only a few materials are necessary and preparation can be done in the car. However, if you have the time, it's a good idea to look over the instructions in advance so you can bring along whatever you'll need. My family likes to put the materials for certain games into separate bags with labels. Whenever we feel like playing, all we have to do is reach for a bag and start right in.

How many games? My family plans one or two games for every hour of traveling time. We also bring along some quiet activities such as cards for solitaire, coloring books, crayons, and picture books for the kids to enjoy on the trip home, when we're usually too tired for organized games.

Variety It's fun to choose several types of games from the different sections of this book. It's also a good idea to alternate high-pitched games with quieter ones to prevent the children from getting overexcited. Of course, your children's ages and interests should be your prime consideration when deciding which games your family would like to play.

Age differences If any of your children are under three, it isn't likely that they will be able to participate in games with much older children. Even the simplest games in this book require some basic skill, such as recognizing and identifying colors, numbers, or letters of the alphabet. However, most of the games in the book can be adjusted a bit to make it possible for children of different ages to compete fairly.

In games requiring specific knowledge or skills, the younger child is at a definite disadvantage. There are a few ways of handling this, depending on the type of game you are playing. You can assign an easier task to the younger child while keeping the rules the same. For example, if you're playing a spelling game, the younger child can be allowed to spell two- or three-letter words, while the older ones must find words of four letters or more. If you're playing a game which requires answering a question or doing a task before moving ahead, gear the questions and tasks to the ages of the children so that each one can play on his own level.

In cases where it's difficult to step down the game for the younger child, you can spot him a few points to even things out. The number of points will depend on the relative ages of your children.

With some games, this may not be necessary. For example, in bingo-type games the four- or five-year-old isn't at any disadvantage as long as he can recognize the markings on his card. If he runs into trouble, an older child can always help him mark his card or show him where to mark it.

Choosing for first The order of play is much more important to children than to adults. Ordinarily, you won't want to make a fuss over who's first, but occasionally, it's fun to vary the method of choosing for first. In fact, you can make choosing the order of the players into a game in itself.

Here are some ideas:

Choosing by age—If you are playing a game of skill, the youngest player should go first and the others should take their turns in order of age.

Choosing by chance—You can use the traditional methods of rolling dice or spinning a spinner.

Picking straws—Cut a drinking straw into as many pieces as you have players, making sure that each piece is a different length. Hold the straws in your fist so that only one end sticks out. The children select straws and the one who draws the longest goes first (the other players follow in size order).

Picking numbers—An adult in the car chooses a number from 1 to 12 and writes it on a small slip of paper. Each child calls a number, and the one who comes closest to the number on the slip goes first, the next closest, second, and so on.

Guessing change—Each child takes a guess at the total amount of loose change you have in your wallet or pocket. The closest guess goes first.

Guessing time—It's easy to lose track of time on a long car trip. Tell the children the time that you began driving, and ask them what time it is now. The one who comes closest goes first.

The suggestions given here for choosing the first can also be used as tie breakers.

Other tips Use spiral notebooks; they can easily be folded to one side, and pages can be torn out, if desired, without ruining the notebook.

When playing with dice in a car, put them into a medium-sized clear glass jar, and replace the lid so they don't get lost. To shoot the dice, just shake the jar.

For games that require dice or a spinner, you can use a deck of standard playing cards instead. Take 1 through 8 of all suits and shuffle well. The players simply take turns picking the cards to determine how many spaces they should move, how many points they receive, how many items they must find in the scenery, and so on. If you like, you can include picture cards to indicate special instructions, such as jacks, lose your next turn; queens, move ahead 5 spaces; kings, double your next score.

Some games require grab bag slips. These can be made easily in the car by tearing a few pages out of a spiral notebook and ripping them up into the necessary number of slips. If you want your slips to hold up for many games, it's a good idea to make them with index cards instead of notebook paper.

Prizes There's a lot more motivation in a game when there's a prize for the winner. "Real" prizes aren't necessary, however, to have fun. One reward for winning a game can be getting to choose the next game or going first in the next round. What I usually do when I've planned a car lunch is to cut the children's sandwiches into quarters and give a quarter to the winner of each round. The first person to win all four pieces gets to pick a dessert from the "dessert bag." Naturally, after one child wins the game, the other children are given the rest of their lunch. If your children are reluctant eaters, this is a great way to get them to finish their whole lunch without complaints. And don't forget to bring along a drink in a thermos to wash down the lunch (bringing along drinks is always a good idea).

If you prefer not to eat lunch while driving, use a small snack as a prize. For example, you can give two pretzels to the winner and one to each of the other players. Other easy snack prizes are crackers, raisins, nuts, or pieces of apple.

If you'd rather not mix eating with playing, try a prize gimmick. For instance, save the cash register tapes from the supermarket, and give each child a medium-length strip. Every time a child wins a round or a game, stick a gold star on the blank side of his strip or draw a star on it. At the end of the day, the child who has collected the longest line of stars gets to be the "five-star general" and earns some small extra privilege—getting to stay up 15 minutes later than his usual bedtime, getting to choose the show that the family watches on television, and so on.

"Lucky bucks" are another easy prize. Cut rectangles out of colored paper, and write "one buck" on some, "five bucks" on others (use a different color for each denomination). The winner of the game gets five bucks, second place, three bucks, and third place, one buck. My kids love accumulating the bucks and seeing who can collect the most by the end of the day.

Children over 10 usually enjoy a game just as much without prizes. The challenge of the competition or of beating their own record at some feat is enough to keep their interest alive.

With a little effort, this book can spark your own ideas for road games. Juggle around a few of my suggestions, add a twist of your own, and you may well invent a family favorite!

Note For the sake of simplicity, I have referred to a player as "he" rather than "he or she." Naturally, all explanations apply to girls as well as boys.

HIGHWAY
2·HOG
OBSERVATION GAMES

A moving vehicle is a unique atmosphere for playing games. Since the scenery is constantly changing, things like license plates, road signs, people in other cars, and a variety of different outside objects provide a family with many new stimuli which can be used in games. As you concentrate on the moving scene, you'll be surprised how much you notice that never caught your eye before.

Here are a few tips to keep in mind:

—If you are playing a game that uses license plates in any way, play only with the cars going in the same direction you are. Cars going in the opposite direction pass by much too quickly and often leave questions about plate numbers, car colors, and so on, that can't be resolved.

—In some places the license plates have only numbers or only letters, rather than a combination of the two. If you are riding through such an area and you need information *not* found on the local plates, use road signs instead.

—If a game requires alphabet slips, be sure to underline the letters M and W and N and Z so they won't be confused with each other.

—Most highway observation games work best in moderate to heavy traffic. If a game doesn't roll smoothly because traffic is too thin, try another which requires fewer cars or use a game from a different section of this book.

I hope you enjoy my family's favorite highway observation games.

The Waving Game

(moderate traffic)

Number of players   2 or more (all games in this chapter require 2 or more players, unless instructions indicate otherwise)

Suggested age   3 and up (the scorekeeper should be at least 7)

Time   15 to 25 minutes

Object   To accumulate the most points by waving to passengers in passing cars and getting them to wave back

Materials   Notebook and felt pen for the scorekeeper, watch to keep time

Preparation   The scorekeeper should hold the following list of car colors and their values in his notebook:

> Gold: 10 points
> White: 8 points
> Red: 6 points
> Green: 4 points
> Blue: 2 points
> Any other color: 1 point

Rules   The youngest child in the car goes first. At the starting signal, he has five minutes to wave to his buddies in the passing cars. If they respond by waving back, the scorekeeper puts a check next to the appropriate car color for each response. For example, if two people in a gold car wave, he puts two checks next to "gold." If one person in a green car waves, he puts one check next to "green." People waving from cars which are not gold, white, red, green, or blue are worth only one point each. After five minutes, when time is called, the first waver adds his score. He gets 10 points for each check next to gold, 8 points for each check next to white, 6 for each check next to red, and so on. When Player One has figured out his total score, another waver takes his turn in the same manner. Write a new list of car colors to score each player.

When all the wavers have taken their turns and have counted up their points, the one with the highest score wins the game.

Adaptation for one player   The single player should play two separate 5-minute games and tally his own score for each one. Then he should flip a coin to determine if he may keep the higher score. If he loses the toss, the Phantom player gets the higher score and wins the game.

Note   To make this game more fun, you can use commercial play money and pay the wavers the correct amount of dollars for the points they accumulate (a dollar per point).

If your gang enjoys waving games, they're sure to love Hollywood Stars in Chapter 7, "Backseat Board Games" (see page 172).

Beaver!

(heavy traffic)

Suggested age   4 and up

Time   15 to 30 minutes

Object   To find the most "beavers" (station wagons) of your assigned color

Materials   A notebook and a different color felt pen or crayon for each player

Preparation   Draw 30 small tally marks on one sheet of paper. Space them far enough apart so that you can circle each one.

Rules   Each player is assigned a common car color. If there are three players or less, each can be assigned two colors.

Every time a player spots a station wagon of *his* color, he yells out his color plus "beaver"—for example, "Blue beaver!" "White beaver!"—and circles one of the tally marks with his color felt pen or crayon (players should circle tally marks consecutively). If, by mistake, a player yells out "beaver" for a station wagon that is *not* his color, the other players may each circle a tally mark.

When all the tally marks have been circled, players count the number of marks they captured (by counting the marks circled with their color) to find their scores. The player who circled the *last* tally mark earns a 5-point bonus. High score wins.

Adaptation for one player   The single player needs a felt pen and notebook to keep score, a watch to keep time, and a paper bag. The player chooses any four common car colors. He plays a separate five-minute round for each color—scoring one point for each station wagon of the proper color. At the end of 20 minutes he will have four scores recorded. He writes the four colors on four slips of paper and puts them into a paper bag. (Children who can't read can simply put a dot of each color on the four slips.) He shakes up the bag, picks out two slips, and then adds together his points for these two colors to determine his score. The sum of the points for the other two colors is the Phantom's score. High score wins.

VARIATION

Put about 30 drinking straws in a cup or container of some kind. Each time a player spots a "beaver" of his color, he takes a straw from the container. If any player calls out a car that is not his color by mistake, he must put a straw back.

When there are no straws left, players count to see who collected the most. The player who picked the last straw gets a 5-point bonus. High score wins the game.

Scenic Names

(light traffic)

Suggested age 7 and up

Time About 20 minutes

Object To find the most things in the scenery whose names begin with the first six letters in your name

Materials Felt pen and notebook for each player

Rules Each child should write the first six letters of his name, spread apart, at the top of his notebook page. If his name has less than six letters, he should add the first letter or two of his last name. Omit duplicate letters as well as letters which would be too difficult to work with (J, K, Q, U, X, Z). Here is one example:

S   **A**   **N**   **D**   **Y**   **B**

At the starting signal, each player gets 15 minutes to write down all the objects (animate or inanimate) he can find in the scenery whose names begin with any of the letters in his name. He may also call out objects that he sees in passing cars. With my name as a sample, here is one possible list:

S	A		N	D	Y	B
sky (1)	airplane (1)	−3	deer (1)	yard (1)	billboard (1)
sun (1)	alley (1)		dead-end sign (1)	yellow jacket (1)	bicycle (1)
street (2)	art supply store (2)		dump truck (2)		barn (2)
soda machine (2)	automobiles (2)		diner (2)		bird (2)
stop sign (3)					boat basin (3)
station wagon (3)					

Score: 35 − 3 = 32

Responses are written in columns underneath the appropriate letters. When time is called, everyone totals his score. Count 1 point for the first two correct responses for any one letter, 2 points for the next two responses for that same letter, and 3 points for each response over four for that letter (see sample game). Players receive a −3 for any letter which has no responses at all. The player with the highest total score wins the game.

Adaptation for one player The single player plays the game the same way. He may check this rating scale to see how well he did:

Under 10 points: Weak
11 to 15 points: Fair
16 to 25 points: Good
26 to 35 points: Very good
35 to 45 points: Excellent
Over 45 points: Expert!

Scenery Sequence

(light traffic)

Suggested age 5 and up

Time 10 to 20 minutes

Object To remember the longest series of objects found in the passing scenery

Rules A player is chosen to start the game. He calls out one object in the passing scenery, such as "tree." The next player says "tree" plus a second object he sees, such as "house." The next player must say "tree," "house," plus one new object, such as "fence." Each succeeding player repeats the *whole* series in order and adds a new object of his own. Eventually, one player will make a mistake in the order. He receives one penalty point, and the next player starts off a new series with a new word. Each time someone forgets the sequence, the round is over, and a new one begins. When a player receives 5 penalty points, he is eliminated. If there are more than two participants, the remaining players continue the game until only *one* player is left. He is the winner.

Adaptation for one player The player calls out one object he sees in the passing scenery. Then he calls the first object plus another one, then the first *two* plus one more, and so on. When he makes a mistake in the sequence, he writes down the number of things he was able to say correctly. He plays three rounds and adds his score. Then he tries another series of three rounds to see if he can improve his score. If so, he wins the game.

Stolen Car

(moderate to heavy traffic)

Suggested age 5 and up

Time 15 to 30 minutes

Object To be the first detective to find 3 stolen cars with thieves

Materials One paper bag, slips of paper with descriptions of "stolen cars," spinner (1–6) or die

Preparation On each slip of paper write the color of the car that was stolen. Choose common colors like red, green, white, yellow, brown, and blue (for 4 players or less, make two slips for each of the colors). Fold each slip, and place in the bag.

Rules Each player picks one car color slip from the bag and shakes the die (or spins the spinner) to determine how many "thieves" must be in the stolen car he is looking for. For example, if the player picks the color blue and rolls a 2, he must look for a blue car with two people. When he finds it, he may pick a new color slip, shoot again, and repeat the procedure. The first player to find three stolen cars with the correct amount of "thieves" wins the game.

If you find that not too many cars with five or six people are appearing, you may eliminate one or both of these numbers and have players shoot again if they get a 5 or a 6.

Adaptation for one player The player looks for three stolen cars with "thieves" in the same manner as described above. He should note the time he began the game and the time he successfully found the last stolen car. How long did it take him to complete his mission? Can he beat his record next time he plays the game?

VARIATION

Missing Persons

Suggested age   4 and up

Time   15 to 30 minutes

Object   To be the first detective to complete 3 assignments successfully (the number of assignments can be increased for a longer game)

Materials   Paper bag with slips of paper that have "missing person" descriptions on them, one die or spinner (numbered 1–6)

Preparation   Write a description of a person on each of several slips of paper (if you are playing three rounds, make up three slips for each player). The slips should say something like this: bald man, man with a beard, man with a moustache, man with blond hair (or grey hair or brown hair), man wearing glasses, woman or girl wearing earrings, girl with braids or pigtails, man or boy wearing a hat, woman wearing something red (or any other color you choose), man wearing something blue (or any other color you choose), and so on. Fold each slip and put them all into the paper bag.

Rules   Each player picks one "missing person" slip from the bag. He then shoots the die (or spins the spinner) to determine how many missing persons he must find that fit the description on his slip. For example, if a player picks "bald man" and shoots a 3, he must look in the passing cars and point out three different bald men in order to complete his assignment. Naturally, they don't all have to be in the same car. Then he reaches into the bag for another slip, shoots the die, and repeats the procedure for a second assignment. The first player to complete three assignments wins the game.

Adaptation for one player The player has 15 minutes to complete as many assignments as he can. He writes down the number completed and then plays a second 15-minute round. Can he complete more assignments the second time around?

Escape From the Road Monster

(moderate to heavy traffic)

Number of players Even number (2, 4, or 6)

Suggested age 5 and up

Time 10 to 20 minutes

Object *For Billy,* to escape before the Road Monster can get him. *For the Road Monster,* to get to Billy and eat him up!

Materials Game picture, eraser or felt pen for each player

Preparation With a *pencil* draw the game picture in one player's notebook. There should be seven ropes tying up Billy and seven hills separating him from the Monster.

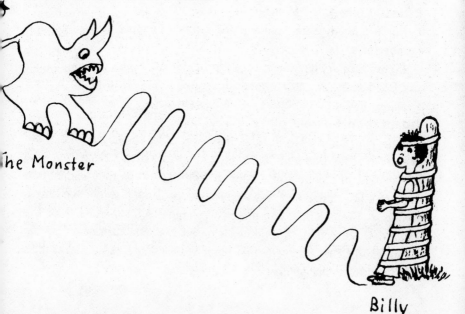

The Monster

Billy

Rules A road monster is on the loose and the Bogeyman has tied up poor little Billy so the Monster can come and eat him up. One player or team will be Billy, and the other player or team, the Road Monster. The player who is Billy looks at the passing license plates to find ones which have two of any number from 0 to 4. The duplicate numbers can be side by side (such as "331") or separated (such as "202"). The Road Monster is on the lookout for plates which have two of any number from 5 to 9, either together or separated. Each time Billy finds a double digit from 0 to 4, he can erase or cross out a loop of rope. Each time the Monster finds a double digit from 5 to 9, he can erase or cross out a hill. Naturally, if you are playing in teams, any team member who spots the double number may call it out.

If the Monster can eliminate all the hills before Billy escapes, the Monster wins the game. On the other hand, if Billy eliminates all his ropes before the Monster reaches him, Billy wins.

Notes If you live in a place that has only numbers on its license plates, you should require the two digits to appear side by side—for example, "005" but not "050."

If you're dealing with all-letter plates, look for licenses which have two of the same letter, together (such as "OOM") or apart (such as "MOM"). Assign half the alphabet (A to M) to Billy and the other half (N to Z) to the Road Monster.

For a longer game, make more ropes and more hills (the same number of each).

If your kids are like mine, they'll probably all want a chance to play the Road Monster. It's a good idea to have a second game picture available and let the players or teams switch roles for a second game.

Adaptation for one player The single player will need a one-minute egg timer. He decides if he wants to be Billy or the Road Monster. The Phantom takes the other position. Each time the player finds the double of a number from 0 to 4, he may eliminate a rope or a hill, depending on which role he is playing. And each time a minute runs out on the egg timer, he eliminates a rope or hill for the Phantom. Of course, the player is on his honor to turn over the egg timer when it runs out. The first player to eliminate all his marks (hills or ropes), wins the game.

Four-Letter Words

(moderate to heavy traffic)

Suggested age   7 and up

Time   15 to 35 minutes

Object   To win the letters you pick by finding them on license plates and be the first player to make three four-letter words

Materials   Commercial letter tiles or a bag of letter slips and a notebook and felt pen to keep score

Preparation   None, if you have commercial letter tiles. Otherwise, make slips of paper for all the letters from A to Z, with three extras each for A, E, I, and O. Put your letter slips (38 in all) into a bag.

Rules   This game is hardly as "racy" as the title suggests! Each player picks an alphabet slip or letter tile from the bag. Players look at passing license plates to find their letters. (The letter must be part of the license number. It can't appear only in the name of the state.) The first player to spot his letter and call it out may keep it, while the other players must put their letters back in the bag. Play continues in this way until one player has won enough letters to make three four-letter words. Players may use their letters in more than one word. For example, if a player has won B, O, R, A, and E, he may use them to form the three words "robe," "bore," and "bear." Note that an S may *not* be used to pluralize three-letter words. Nor are proper nouns, slang words, and abbreviations permitted. The first player to form three different four-letter words with his accumulated letters wins the game.

Note   Six-year-olds can participate in this game if you allow them to make three-letter words. Older children may prefer the challenge of forming five- or six-letter words.

Adaptation for one player   Follow the above rules, and time yourself to see how long it takes to form three four-letter words. Play another round to see if you can improve your time.

Something in Common

(moderate to heavy traffic)

Suggested age   6 and up

Time   20 minutes

Object   To find the most cars which have something in common with your own

Materials   Notebook and felt pen for the scorekeeper, watch to keep time

Preparation   None

Rules   Before the game begins, the scorekeeper should write the name of each player, including himself, in his notebook. Each time any player calls out an acceptable similarity, he should put a tally mark next to that player's name. After 15 minutes, when "time" is called, the scorekeeper counts the points made by each player. The one with the most points wins the game.

At the starting signal, the players have 15 minutes to look at the passing cars and passengers to find things which they have in common with their own car and passengers. To give you an idea of the wide range of possibilities, here are seven of the responses which my son gave when we played this game:

> Our car is yellow, and so is that one.
> The man in that car has curly hair, just like Daddy.
> That car has four doors, just like ours.
> The lady in that car is wearing a red blouse, and so is my mother.
> That car is a station wagon, just like ours.
> That driver has his front window open, just like Daddy.
> Our car has black seat covers, and so does that one.

The responses which players call out can cover any detail of car or passengers. However, there are a couple of ground rules.

First, no player can call out a similarity which is common to *all* cars. For example, the player could not say, "That car has four wheels, just like ours." However, he could say, "That car has white-wall tires, just like ours."

Second, no player can call out a similarity previously given by another player. For example, if one player has already said, "That car has two adults and two children, like ours," another player couldn't say the same thing about passengers in a different car. However, he could say, "That car has two males and two females, just like ours," since the sex of the passengers was not mentioned by the previous player.

Adaptation for one player The single player should follow the same procedure outlined above and tally his own responses. At the end of 15 minutes, he can check this rating scale and see how well he fared:

Less than 5 similarities: Poor
6 to 10 similarities: Fair
11 to 15 similarities: Good
16 to 20 similarities: Very good
21 or more similarities: Excellent!

Moving Advertisements

(heavy traffic)

Suggested age   7 and up

Time   15 to 30 minutes

Object   To be the first player to spot three of the same type of advertisement on moving vehicles (this game has to be played on a road that allows commercial vehicles)

Materials   Notebook and felt pen for each player

Rules Players look at passing vehicles to spot ones with advertisements or store titles on them. The ads can be on trucks, buses, vans, taxis, or even cars (on bumper stickers for resorts or tourist attractions). Any time a player spots an ad, he calls it out and writes it down in his notebook. Players should group the moving ads according to type: food or drinks, furniture stores, moving vans, sightseeing attractions, and so on. If two players call out the same ad simultaneously, play stops and they flip a coin to see who will get it. The first player to find and record three of the same type of ad wins the game.

VARIATION

Players look for ads for 15 minutes. Instead of recording the type of ad, they record the type of vehicle they find it on. When time is called, players score 2 points for each ad found on a truck or bus and 3 points for each one found on a taxi or car. Points are added up, and the player with the highest total wins.

Back and Forth Alphabet Signs

(moderate traffic)

Number of players 2

Suggested age 5 and up (or younger if the child can recognize the letters of the alphabet in sequence)

Time 15 to 30 minutes

Object To be the first player to reach the other end of the alphabet by finding the letters he needs on road signs

Rules Each player is assigned one end of the alphabet. The younger child should begin at A and the older child at Z. The younger child must spot a road sign of any kind that contains the letter A. He calls out that letter and then looks for a sign that contains the letter B.

When he find a B, he may go on to C, and so forth. The older child begins by finding a sign that contains the letter Z. When he finds one, he calls out that letter and may go on to Y, then X, then W, and so on—going through the alphabet backward. The first player to reach his end of the alphabet wins the game.

If the older child has difficulty recalling the sequence of the alphabet in reverse, an adult can write down the letters for him.

Note My family has found that the letters Q and Z are much more difficult to find than the others. Therefore, for those two letters *only*, we permit the players to use license plate letters.

Adaptation for one player Record the time it takes to find all letters of the alphabet from A to Z. Now try it backward, from Z to A. Can you finish as quickly going in the opposite direction?

VARIATION

Back and Forth License Numbers

Instead of assigning the two ends of the alphabet to the two players or teams, assign opposite ends of the number scale from 0 to 9. It's best to let the younger player go from low to high. The players look for the numbers on passing license plates rather than on road signs and call them out in the sequence assigned to them. The first player to reach the opposite end of the number scale wins. Follow the same adaptation for one player as in the standard game, substituting numbers for letters.

Road Bingo

(moderate traffic)

Suggested age 5 and up

Time 20 to 30 minutes

Object To get five boxes on the bingo card in a line in any direction—vertically, horizontally, or diagonally. Other goals could be filling in the border around the card, checkerboard bingo (every other square, starting with the square in the upper left hand corner), an X (both directions diagonally), other letters of the alphabet (T, L, E, or F), or even the whole card.

Materials Notebook and felt pen for each player

Preparation Each player draws a bingo card with 25 squares (five across and five down) and writes any one-digit number he wishes in each of the squares. Zero (0) is included as a one-digit number since it does appear on license plates. Adults can draw up cards for children who cannot draw their own. (Make sure all the cards have a different arrangement of numbers or everyone will get bingo at the same time.)

5	2	4	8	0
3	7	9	4	8
8	1	5	3	2
6	0	6	7	0
5	9	8	1	5

Rules One person in the car, preferably someone who isn't playing, is the caller. The children can also take turns being the caller. Every time a car passes, the caller shouts out the first number on the license plate. Each player may cross out that number on his card in one place only. The game continues until a player gets bingo.

VARIATIONS

Two-Digit Number Bingo (ages 6 and up)

Write two-digit numbers on the cards and have the caller shout out the first *two* numbers on the plates (this game takes about 15 minutes longer to play).

Alphabet Bingo (ages 4 and up)

Write letters of the alphabet in each square. The caller shouts out the first *letter* to appear on a passing license plate. For each call players cross out that letter in one place only. My children prefer this version to Number Bingo.

Color Bingo (ages 3 and up)

Draw a big dot of color in each square. The caller shouts out things in the passing scenery of different colors: *green* grass, *blue* sky, *red* barn, *brown* tree trunk, and so on. Colors can be repeated on the card (repeats are allowed in *all* versions of bingo) but can be crossed out in only one place for each call.

Plus One or Minus One Bingo (ages 6 and up)

These games are more challenging for children who are tired of the usual versions of bingo. For Plus One Bingo, write any digit from 1 through 10 in each of the 25 boxes. When the caller shouts out the first number on a plate (zero is a legitimate call), the players must silently add one to that number and cross out the number that is *one more* than the number called. For example, if the caller says "5," the players would cross out 6.

For Minus One Bingo, make up the cards with the numbers −1, 0, 1, 2, and so on, through 8. When the caller shouts out the first number on the license plate, the players must cross out a number that is one less. For example, if the caller says "zero," players must mark −1. Keep a record of the numbers called to make sure that no one slips. You can also play Plus Two or Minus Two Bingo.

First-Letter or Last-Letter Bingo   (ages 6 and up)

Write a letter of the alphabet in each square. The caller shouts out an object in the passing scenery—for example, "mountain." If you are playing First-Letter Bingo, players would cross out the letter M in one place. In Last-Letter Bingo they would cross out an N (if they had one, of course). In cases where the last letter cannot be heard—for example, in the word "house"—children who cannot yet spell accurately can be told the correct letter to cross out.

Car Bingo   (ages 7 and up)

For this version make a slightly different card, with a total of 36 boxes, six across and six down.

Black out the box in the upper left-hand corner. In the top horizontal column, players write any make of car they wish— Cadillac, Ford, Chevrolet, Buick, Oldsmobile, Dodge, Plymouth, Chrysler, Volkswagen. In the first vertical column, write a common car color—white, red, blue, green, yellow, brown. (If players choose the same makes and colors, they should be sure to vary the order so that they don't all get bingo at the same time).

	Ford	Cadillac	Dodge	Buick	Plymouth
Yellow					
Green					
Blue				X	
White					
Brown					

The caller shouts out the make and color of a passing car—for example, "blue Buick." If a player has chosen Buick as one of his car makes and blue as one of his colors, he moves his felt pen across the blue line until he sees Buick at the top of the column and then puts an X in that box. The first player to get five in a line in any direction wins.

Road Treasure Hunt

(light traffic)

Suggested age   4 and up

Time   15 to 30 minutes

Object   To be the first player to locate all ten items on his list

Materials   Notebook and felt pen for each player

Preparation   In each player's notebook make a list of ten different objects to be found as you drive along. If a child can't read, draw ten simple pictures for his list. The kind of objects to include are listed below. Take one or two from each category for each list. Naturally, the lists should reflect the kind of scenery you might pass on your trip. Therefore, for example, don't include farm-related items if you expect to do city driving, and so on.

Farms: Barn, chicken, horse, cow, tractor, silo, haystack, crops

Transportation: Railroad train, bus, trailer truck, taxicab, garbage truck, fire engine, police car, motorcycle, bicycle, baby carriage, airplane, helicopter, station wagon, van, boat

Stores and commercial enterprises: Supermarket, bank, drug store, book store, toy store, clothing store, gas station, drive-in movie, movie theater, bowling alley, miniature golf course, pizza parlor, pet store, grocery store, diner, fast food outlet (Burger King, McDonald's)

Road signs and signals: Red light, green light, yellow light, signs of all kinds—speed limit: 55, stop, school crossing, merging traffic, yield, exit, dead end, slippery when wet, one way

Types of buildings: shingle house, brick house, church, apartment building, school, hospital, library, garage

Natural features: Tree, grass, flower, mountain, lake, cliff

Miscellaneous items: Fire hydrants, mailboxes, bridges, dogs, parking lots, double-parked cars, flags, smokestacks

Rules Each child receives a list of ten objects. Every time he spots an item on his list, he calls it out and crosses it off his list. The first person to find everything on his list wins the game.

There should be a 15-minute time limit for this game, since occasionally everyone gets hung up on one or two items and the game begins to drag. At the end of 15 minutes, if no one has completed his list, the player who has found the most items on his list wins the game.

Adaptation for one player The child receives a list with seven items to find. (An adult should make up two lists of seven items each.) He records the time it takes him to find all the items on his list (the time limit is 10 minutes; if all items are not found in 10 minutes, he records his score at the end of that time). Now he tries a list with seven *new* items. Can he beat his previous time?

Tally Taking

(moderate to heavy traffic; best played on roads which permit commercial vehicles)

Suggested age 5 and up (children over 7 should help the younger ones with scoring)

Time 15 to 30 minutes

Object To tally up the greatest number of different vehicles within the time limit

Materials   Felt pen and notebook for each player

Preparation   Each player should copy the list shown here into his notebook.   You may want to alter the point values on the list, assigning the lowest ones to the vehicles most commonly seen in the area you're driving in and the highest ones to the vehicles least often seen.   You can also compile your own list.

Two-tone car: 2 points
Motorcycle: 3 points
Trailer truck: 2 points
Station wagon: 2 points
Airplane: 7 points
Van: 2 points
Bus: 4 points
Police car: 10 points
Taxicab: 4 points
Mobile home: 5 points
Train: 5 points
Boat (in water or on carrier): 4 points
Tractor: 8 points
Helicopter: 7 points
Bicycle (being ridden or on carrier): 5 points

Rules   The best way to play this game without confusion is for one person to play at a time.   The first player—Player One—hands his notebook to one of the other players.   Player One has five minutes to find and call out any of the vehicles on the list. (He may look at the list if he forgets what they are.) The player who is holding the notebook checks one of the items for each vehicle that Player One calls.   If Player One gets 10 checks for any one item by spotting 10 vehicles of that type, he receives a bonus of 20 points, in addition to his regular score for that row.   After five minutes, time is called, and Player One adds up his score for each row.   For example, if he spotted two motorcycles (marked by two checks) and motorcycles are worth 3 points each, he would receive 6 points for that row $(2 \times 3 = 6)$.   Add up the points for the other rows in the same manner. Include a bonus of 20 points for each row of 10 or more checks.

After Player One finishes his turn, the other participants play the game in the same way, one by one. The player who gets the highest score for his five minutes of play wins the game.

Adaptation for one player The single player should play this game for 10 minutes, tallying his own scores. Then he should try another 10-minute round, using the variation which follows. Can he better his score the second time around?

VARIATION

Passenger Tally

This variation is played in the same way as the standard version. In this game, however, you collect points by observing specific things about the *passengers* in other cars. Use the list below or make up your own list and play one person at a time as in the standard version. Note that no more than one item can be recorded for each passing car. Thus, if a player spots a car with a curly-haired man wearing yellow, he can record only one of these items on the list.

Man with hat: 5 points
Woman with glasses: 2 points
Man with beard: 3 points
Girl or woman laughing: 10 points
Man with curly hair: 2 points
Woman with gray hair: 2 points
Man or boy laughing: 10 points
Man with mustache: 3 points
Car with five or more people: 4 points
Car with dog (live or stuffed): 7 points
Woman wearing blue: 3 points
Bald man: 8 points
Girl or woman with pigtails or braids: 5 points
Man wearing yellow: 3 points
Car with three or more children: 4 points

Follow the Dots

(light to moderate traffic)

Number of players Even number (2, 4, or 6)

Suggested age 6 and up

Time 15 to 30 minutes

Object To be the first player or team to complete a dot picture

Materials In each player or team's notebook, draw a dot picture with the same number of dots (commercially made dot pictures can be used), felt pen for each player, standard spinner (numbered 1 to 6), or a die in a clear glass jar

Preparation Copy the pattern shown into two notebooks or use ready-made dot pictures.

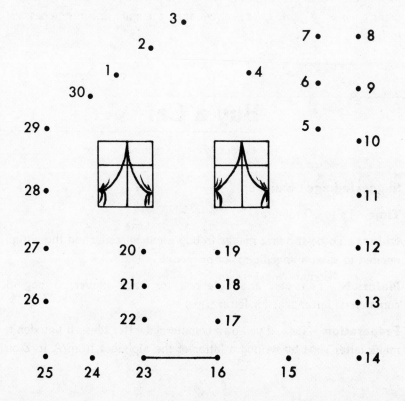

Rules Designate the two players (or teams) as *odd* and *even*. The odd player must look for license plates on which the final digit is odd (1, 3, 5, 7, or 9). The even player must look for plates on which the final digit is even (0, 2, 4, 6, or 8).

At the starting signal, the players look for their assigned numbers. When the odd player spots his first correct number, he calls out "odd—1," then proceeds to "odd—2" and "odd—3." At the same time the even player calls out "even—1," "even—2," and so on. The first player (or team) to spot three correct numbers wins the round and earns the right to spin the spinner and connect that number of dots on his picture, beginning at dot 1. For example, if a 2 is spun, the player draws two lines: one from 1 to 2 and a second from 2 to 3.

As soon as the dots have been connected, the signal is given for the next round, and the players again look for and call out three plates which end in their type of digit. If a player makes a mistake, his opponent automatically wins that round. The winner of Round 2 gets to spin and connect more dots. The first player to connect his entire picture wins the game (an exact count on the spinner is not necessary to finish).

Buy a Car

(moderate to heavy traffic)

Suggested age   8 and up

Time   15 to 30 minutes

Object   To be the first player to buy a car by collecting the letters needed to spell a specific make or model

Materials   Felt pen and notebook for each player, a bag of commercial letter tiles (or letter slips)

Preparation   None, if you own commercial letter tiles. If you don't, make letter slips by writing a letter of the alphabet from A to Z on each of 26 slips of paper. Put the slips into a paper bag and shuffle them well.

Rules Players try to buy a car by collecting letters needed to spell a specific make or model (not in the proper sequence). The car name may be a make or a specific model—(Lincoln) Continental, (Buick) Skylark, (Ford) Pinto, and so on. Here's a sample list of car makes:

Ford	Chrysler	Volkswagen	Lincoln
Plymouth	Toyota	Cadillac	Oldsmobile
Mercury	Datsun	Buick	Rolls Royce
Dodge	Chevrolet	Pontiac	Jaguar

To begin the game, each player picks a letter tile or slip from the bag. Now everyone looks for a make or model of car whose name contains the letter he picked. For example, if a player picked the letter C, he would look for a Cadillac, a Lincoln, or a Chevrolet or a model name such as Continental or Wildcat. The first player to call out a car make or model with his letter writes that letter in his notebook. Then everyone (including the winner of the round) puts his letter back into the bag, and the next round begins. In each round, the player who first spots a car whose name contains his letter gets to write that letter down. The first player to collect all the letters needed to spell a car or model name wins the game. The other players may continue playing for second place, third place, and so on.

It's possible for a player to collect more letters than the amount needed to spell one car name. For example, one player may collect R S O P L F N D, and then unscramble four of those to spell FORD. There is no penalty for leftover letters. However, if two players complete a car name on the same turn, the one with the fewest extra letters is the winner.

Adaptation for one player The single player sets a time limit for himself, perhaps 15 minutes. Each time he picks a letter, he must find a car make or model with that letter before he may write it down. If he does not find his letter after a minute or two, he may choose to put it back and pick another, so as not to waste time. If he gathers the letters needed to spell any one car name within the time limit, he wins the game.

Highway Bowling

(moderate traffic)

Suggested age   7 and up

Time   30 to 45 minutes

Object   To bowl the highest score

Materials   Slips in a paper bag, a notebook and felt pen for each player, a one-minute egg timer or watch with a second hand

Preparation   For this game you will need ten slips in your paper bag for each player in the game. Twenty-six of them can be the letters from A to Z. Ten of them can be numbers from 0 to 9. If you need more slips, you can label them as certain colors (red, blue, green, white, yellow, brown, gold). Or, if you like, use a mixture of letter, number, and color slips. Put all the slips into a paper bag and toss around well.

Each player should draw a bowling scorecard with ten frames into his notebook. For a shorter game, you can play only five frames. (In bowling each round is called a frame.)

1	2	3	4	5	6	7	8	9	10	TOTAL

Rules   Choose to see who will go first. To begin the tournament, the first player chooses a slip from the bag. If it is a letter or number, he has one minute to find that letter or number on as many different license plates or road signs as possible (only one letter or number a plate or sign is allowed). If it's a color, he has one minute to point out that color on (or in) as many different cars or other objects in the passing scenery as possible.

Let's say he picks the letter D and finds ten or more licenses or signs with the letter D within one minute. The player scores a strike and may record 20 points in his first frame box (he should *not* put the D back into the paper bag). However, if the player finds fewer than 10 D's in one minute, he gets one more chance to score a total of 10, as in regular bowling. He plays a second one-minute round using the same letter. If he succeeds in finding a total of 10 or more D's in both turns combined, he has bowled a spare and scores 15 points in his first frame. Of course, there will be some occasions when a player spots fewer than 10 items in two turns. If this is the case, he simply writes the total number of correct answers (a 9 or less) in the first box.

When the first player has finished frame 1, the other players take their turns in the same manner. Then players go on to frames 2, 3, 4, 5, and so on. Never return used slips to the bag.

Scoring   The scores are totaled as you go along. That is, if the player whose scorecard is shown got a strike in frame 1 (scoring 20 points) and scored 9 in frame 2, he would write the total of both of these scores in the second frame box (20 + 9 = 29).

1	2	3	4	5	6	7	8	9	10	TOTAL
20	29	44	50	65	85	93	102	122	127	127

If he got a spare on his third turn (scoring 15 points), he would add 15 to 29 and write that total (44) in frame 3. Players total their scores in this manner until they have completed all 10 frames. The player with the highest score wins.

Adaptation for one player   The single player plays the game exactly as described above, trying to come as close as he can to a perfect score of 200 (or 100, for the shortened five-frame version).

Scoring variation   This game can be scored exactly like regular bowling, with a possible high score of 300. I won't go into the more complicated scoring of standard bowling here, but if you are bowlers, you may want to use that scoring method.

Winner!

(moderate traffic)

Suggested age   7 and up (players must be able to spell 3-letter words)

Time   15 to 30 minutes

Object   To spell as many 3-letter words in sequence as possible in 5 minutes, using the letters on passing plates

Materials   Notebook and felt pen for scoring, watch to keep time

Rules   One person at a time plays this game while another records letters and keeps score for him. At the starting signal, the player who is up calls out a letter on a passing plate to be the first letter in his word. Now he must look for and call out a second letter for that word. Let's suppose the first two letters he calls are F and I. The third letter he calls must complete a three-letter word beginning with FI. Some good choices might be the letters N, T, or X. The player should be careful to avoid letter combinations that can be completed in only one way. He can't use more than one letter per license plate, nor can he change the order of letters once he's called them.

When a player has completed a legitimate three-letter word, he wins the first letter in the word "winner," the W, and begins searching for a new three-letter word in sequence as above.   When he completes a second word, he wins the second letter in the word "winner" (the I), and so on.

Opponents may challenge a word they think is incorrect. If the player is wrong he doesn't win another letter of "winner" and begins a new word. However, if the challenger is wrong, the player wins an *extra* letter. Naturally, time out is called during a challenge.

After five minutes, the player's turn is up and another player takes his turn (incomplete words receive no credit). When all players have gone, the one who came the closest to collecting all the letters in the word "winner" wins the game.

If no one has spelled "winner" by the end of round one, players can play a second five-minute round. If a player gets "winner" in the second round before his time is up, he should continue playing for the numbers 1, 2, 3, and so on.

Adaptation for one player The single player should time how long it takes him to collect all the letters in "winner." Another day he may want to try to beat his own record.

VARIATION

Greedy Ghost Grab Bag Game

Suggested age 7 and up (children must be able to spell 3-letter words)

Time 15 to 30 minutes

Object To collect the most points from the grab bag while avoiding the Greedy Ghost

Materials Grab bag slips in paper bag, felt pen, notebook for each player

Preparation You will need 25 slips of paper which you can easily make by tearing two or three notebook pages into smaller pieces. On seven of them, draw the Greedy Ghost (or GG, if you prefer). The rest of the 18 slips should be distributed this way: five slips with the number 5, four slips with the number 10, three slips with the number 15, three slips with the number 20, and three slips with the number 25. Put all 25 slips into a paper bag and shake well.

Rules All players attempt to make a three-letter word at the same time. As in Winner!, they spot and call out three letters on three different license plates. A player should plan his strategy carefully because once he has chosen a letter, he can't change his mind and he can't change the order of the letters. He should try to choose combinations which can end in several different ways.

The first player to complete a word shows it to the others, and if it's legitimate and correctly spelled, he wins the right to grab for points from the bag. If a player's word is not legitimate or is incorrectly spelled, he is eliminated from that round and the remaining players continue to look for words. If there are only two players in the game, the opponent automatically wins the round.

The winner of the round may now pick a score slip from the grab bag. Let's say that the first slip he picks is the number 10. At this point he has the choice to either stop and record that number as his score *or* to take a risk and pick again. As long as the player continues to pick numbers, he can increase his score for the round. However, he shouldn't be too greedy, for if he picks a Greedy Ghost, he loses all the points he has accumulated on that turn, and the next round begins. If a player grabs the Greedy Ghost on his first pick, he doesn't receive any score for that round.

Play additional rounds in the same manner. Each time a player is first to form a three-letter word, he wins the right to grab from the bag. (Time out is always called when a player is picking for scores.) Whenever a new round begins, players must cross out the letters they collected from the previous round and start all over again. When all the slips in the bag are used up, the player with the highest score wins. If children over 8 or 9 years of age are playing with children of 6 or 7, the older ones should be required to find four-letter words while younger ones are looking for words of three letters. This will even out the age gap.

Adaptation for one player For the single player, you will need only 14 slips for the grab bag: three slips with the Greedy Ghost picture, three 5-point slips, three 10-point slips, two 15-point slips, two 20-point slips, and one 25-point slip. Each time the player forms a three-letter word he may grab from the bag. When all the slips are used up, the player can look at this chart to see how well he did:

Under 40: Greed does not pay!
40 to 60: Still a little too greedy
65 to 80: Good job
85 to 100: Very sharp
Over 100: Great!

The Closer the Better

(light to moderate traffic)

Suggested age 9 and up, depending on the players' ability to add and subtract three-digit numbers

Time 15 to 30 minutes

Object To win the highest point scores by arranging your license numbers so they come as close as possible to the numbers you shoot on the dice

Materials Notebook and felt pen for each player, pair of dice in clear glass jar

Rules Each player is assigned a car color. Choose common colors such as red, blue, green, white. When the first car of his color passes, each player records the first three numerals (0 through 9) that appear on the license plate. When all players have recorded three digits, one of them shakes the dice.

The value of each dice combination is as follows:

> Total of 2: 200
>
> Total of 3: 300
>
> Total of 4: 400
>
> Total of 5: 500
>
> Total of 6: 600
>
> Total of 7: 700
>
> Total of 8: 800
>
> Total of 9: 900
>
> Total of 10: 1000
>
> Total of 11: 100
>
> Total of 12: high number wins

Let's say the total is five. A glance at the table shows that 5 stands for 500. Each player must now arrange his three numerals into a number which is as close as possible to 500. Let us look at the digits of two hypothetical players:

Player A   **Player B**

0 3 6   1 4 2

Player A should rearrange his numbers to read 603, since this is the closest he can come to 500 (103 away from it). Player B should rearrange his numbers to read 421, which is only 79 away from 500.

Now the players look at the Point Value Chart below to record their first-round scores, based on how close they came to 500. In this case, Player A will get 25 points for coming within 150 of 500, and Player B will get 50 points for coming within 100 of it.

Each round is played in the same manner. The players record three more digits from cars of their color, and then one of them shakes the dice. After rearranging their numerals to come as close as possible to the number thrown, they check the Point Value Chart to determine their scores for that round.

Point Value Chart

Exact match: 500 points

Within 25 (higher or lower): 250 points

Within 50 (higher or lower): 100 points

Within 100 (higher or lower): 50 points

Within 150 (higher or lower): 25 points

Within 200 (higher or lower): 15 points

Within 250 (higher or lower): 10 points

More than 250 (higher or lower): No score

High number wins: Winner gets 100 points;

no one else scores

Whenever a 12 (high number wins) is thrown, the game is slightly different. In this instance each player arranges his three numerals to form the highest number possible. The player who can form the highest three-digit number gets 100 points, and the other players don't score in that round. Play 10 rounds in all—seven for a shorter game—and add up the scores. The player with the highest score wins.

Adaptation for one player The only difference in the game for the single player is when his dice total 12. In this case, if he can arrange his numerals to form a number higher than 500, he adds 50 points to his score. If he can only make a number lower than 500, he loses 50 points. If he is able to make *exactly* 500, he gets 500 points for the round. At the end of 10 rounds, the player totals his score and checks this rating scale:

> 150 or less: Weak
> 151 to 250: Fair
> 251 to 350: Good
> 351 to 500: Very good
> 501 to 750: Excellent
> Over 750: Expert!

VARIATION

The Further the Better

The object of this game is to arrange your three numerals to form a number which is *as far as possible* from the number on the dice. Use the Point Value Chart below to determine the scores for each round. After 10 rounds the player with the highest total wins.

Adaptation for one player The same as the adaptation for The Closer the Better, except that the player is trying to arrange his numbers to get as *far* as possible from the number he throws.

Point Value Chart
> 500 or more (higher or lower): 250 points
> 400 or more (higher or lower): 100 points
> 350 or more (higher or lower): 75 points
> 300 or more (higher or lower): 50 points
> 250 or more (higher or lower): 25 points
> 200 or more (higher or lower): 15 points
> 150 or more (higher or lower): 10 points
> Closer than 150 (higher or lower): No score
> High number wins: Winner gets 100 points;
> no one else scores

Jumbled Letters

(light traffic)

Suggested age 9 and up

Time 15 to 45 minutes, depending on the number of rounds played

Object To win the most points by making the greatest number of words which contain the first three letters on a license plate

Materials Notebook and felt pen or crayon for each player

Rules One person in the car is chosen to be the caller (or children can take turns being the caller). To begin round one, the caller shouts out the first three letters that appear on any passing license plate. Everyone writes down the letters and has five minutes (or 5 miles of traveling distance on the odometer) to write down as many words as he can which contain those three letters—and any additional letters—in *any* order. For example, if the letters called are E, T, and A, some possible words are "eat," "tea," "tear," "rate," "treat," "date," "seat," "entrance." No proper nouns, abbreviations, or slang words are permitted. A word can be used in only one form on any given list; therefore, if a player uses the word "starts," he may not use "started," "start," "starting," and so on. At the end of the designated time limit, everybody adds up his score. Three-letter words score 3 points, four-letter words, 4 points, five-letter words, 5 points, six-letter words, 6 points, seven-letter words or more, 10 points. If a player spells a word incorrectly, he does not receive credit for it. Thus, each person has a score for round one. Play two to four more rounds, depending on how long you want the game to be. At the end of three, four, or five rounds, the player with the highest score wins.

If children seven to nine years of age would like to compete with older kids, they can do so fairly by only having to make words which contain the *first two* letters on the license plate. Six-year-olds may also be able to play if they are permitted to make words only using the first letter.

Adaptation for one player The player tries three rounds of this game and sees whether he can better his score each time.

Highway Hopscotch

(moderate to heavy traffic)

Suggested age 8 and up

Time 20 to 40 minutes

Object To capture numbers along the hopscotch path

Materials Hopscotch path and score sheet, felt pen for each player, spinner numbered 1–6 or die in clear glass jar, and watch with second hand or two-minute egg timer

Preparation Draw the hopscotch path shown here into one player's notebook

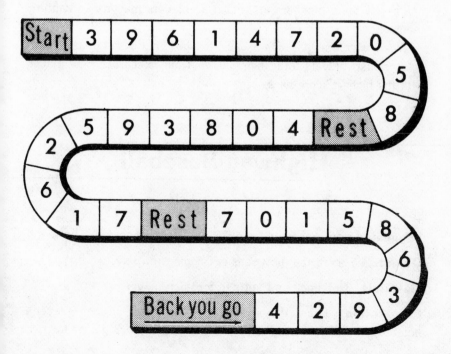

Rules The first player shoots the die, and beginning at start moves the number of spaces indicated, and writes his first name outside the box where he lands. Let's say he lands on the number 4. This gives him the chance to win that number *everywhere* it appears along the path. To do so, he shoots the die again, say a 3. He now has two minutes to find the number 4 on *three* different license plates. If he succeeds, he may write his initials inside *every* box with the number 4. However, if he fails, the box remains free. The next player goes in the same manner.

Whenever a player lands on a number owned by another player, he must write −5 underneath his name on the score sheet. When a player lands on a number he's already captured on the path, he writes +5 underneath his name on the score sheet. In a rest box, he does nothing. When players reach the end of the path (exact count is not necessary) they go back toward start on their next turn. On the return trip, players should write their age outside the box they land on, so they won't confuse these moves with their previous ones (if children are the same age, use another identification such as middle name). If some numbers are still free, players may try to capture them.

When *everyone* has come back to start (it doesn't matter who returns first) players total their plus and minus scores. The player with the highest score wins.

Highway Baseball

(moderate traffic)

Suggested age 8 and up (an older child or adult should keep score)

Object To score the most runs in 5 innings of play

Materials Notebook and felt pen for each player

Preparation Draw the scorecard shown here in one player's notebook. The scorecard here is for a three-player game; for two players you would have only two rows, for four players, four, and so on.

	1	2	3	4	5
Player One					
Player Two					
Player Three					

Rules Choose to see which player will be up first. The first player at bat looks at the passing cars to find license plates with the letter S for a *single*, D for a *double*, T for a *triple*, or H for a *home run*. When the player spots any one of these letters, he calls it out and writes it in his notebook. He must write the letters in the order in which he spots them.

As he is doing this, his opponents are on the lookout for out-of-state plates, MD plates, or plates with the letter or numeral O. Any time an opponent spots one of these three plates, the player at bat receives *one out*. Opponents must spot three such plates (for three outs) in order to retire Player One for that inning.

There are a few important points to remember. First, an out-of-state or out-of-province plate is one which does not come from the state or province you are driving in. Therefore, if your car is from New York, but you are driving in California, all plates but California ones are considered out of state, including New York plates. Also, any one license plate can be used for only one play. For instance, if a plate number reads 123–DSL, the player who is up may call out a double or a single, but not both (he will obviously want to choose a double). Or if a plate has two 0's, opponents may call just one of them to make an out against the player at bat. By the same token, if one license plate contains both a scoring letter (S, D, T, or H) and an O, such as 102–HRB, the player who spots that plate first is the only one allowed to use it. For example, if the player at bat calls out the H before his opponents call out the O, they can't use that license plate to score an out against the batter. (The reverse is also true.)

This game should be played only with cars going in the same

direction as your car. Cars heading in the opposite direction pass too fast, which may lead to unresolvable arguments about what letters and numbers appeared on a license.

After the opposing team calls three outs, Player One totals his score, and the next player is up. I have scored one inning to show you how to do it. Note that the runners do not advance any extra bases, but go one base if the batter hits a single, two if he hits a double, and so on. A man has to circle the bases and get back to home plate to score a run. You can follow the action on the baseball diamond illustrated. Player One's first inning score is S S S H T D H T. Here's how it plays:

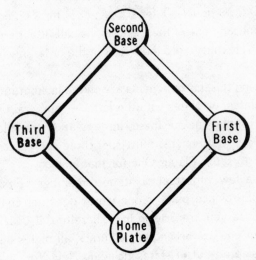

S—Player One scores a *single*. There is now a man on first base.

S—With a new man up, he scores another *single*. The man on first base advances to second and the man who hit the single is on first. There are now men on first and second.

S—Player One scores a third *single*. All runners advance one base. The bases are now loaded.

H—Player One hits a *home run*. As his man circles the bases, he scores all the other men ahead of him—a *grand slam*. Since all four men cross home plate, Player One scores 4 runs.

The opposing team calls *one out*.

T—Player One's next batter gets a triple, so there is now a man on third.

D—The next batter hits a *double*. The man on third scores (making a total, thus far, of 5 runs), and there is a man on second. The opposing team calls the *second out*.

H—The next batter up hits a *home run*. The man on second scores, as does the man who hit the homer. Player One now has 7 runs.

T—The next batter up hits a *triple*. At this point, an opponent calls the *third out*. Since the man on third base never makes it home, this last triple doesn't result in any score.

Player One's first inning total is 7 runs, so he writes a 7 in his first inning box.

The remaining players take turns playing the first inning and scoring runs in the same manner. The game goes on for five innings. There may be innings when three outs are called before a player can score any runs. In this case, his score for that inning is zero. When all players have completed five innings, total each player's score. The player with the most runs wins the game. In the case of a tie, play extra innings as in regular baseball.

Secret Word Contest

(moderate traffic)

Suggested age 8 and up

Time 15 to 30 minutes

Object To guess the other player's word before he can guess yours

Materials Notebook and felt pen or crayon for each player

Rules Each player writes down a secret five-letter word on a page of his notebook, hiding it from the other players. Players turn to the next page of their notebooks and write down the names of all the other players in the game. Choose to see who will go first. The first player calls out any letter he sees on a passing license plate—for example, T. If any player in the car besides the caller has a T, he must say, "I have one" or "I have two," as the case may be. (He doesn't have to reveal the position of the letter.) Players write a T (or two T's) next to the names of each player who has one. They should also write the letter T at the top of their pages so as not to call it again. If anyone in the car has the letter the caller chose, he may go again. Otherwise his turn is over, and the next player takes a turn as caller. Eventually, players will have collected enough letters next to each player's name to guess what the other players' secret words might be. A player may then use his turn to guess someone else's word. If he doesn't guess the word, play continues as before. If he is correct, however, he is the winner of the round. The first player to win three rounds is the winner.

For a more difficult game, use six- or seven-letter secret words; for an easier one, use three- or four-letter words. The only requirement is that all players choose words with the same number of letters.

Adaptation for one player The player writes down any five-letter word in his notebook. Let's say he choses the word "smart." He has 5 minutes to find the letters in his word on the passing license plates. He must find and cross them off in order. At the end of 5 minutes, the player scores one point for each letter he found. Play three rounds, thinking of a new five-letter word each time. A perfect score is 15.

Turn Over Triplets

(moderate traffic)

Suggested age 7 and up (see variation for a similar game which can be played with children 4 and up)

Time 15 to 30 minutes

Object To be the first player to pick three identical pictures

Materials Paper bag with picture slips

Preparation Tear a few pages out of a spiral notebook, and cut them into 30 slips. Make three slips for each of the simple pictures shown here or for any easy pictures, shapes, letters, or numbers you wish. However, you must include three wild cards.

Rules An adult or older child who is not participating (or even the driver) should call out a simple addition or subtraction problem whose answer is a number from 0 to 9. For example, "4 + 5" or 13 – 4." Now (without speaking) all players must look on the passing plates for the answer to the problem. The first player to spot the answer on a plate and call it out gets to pick a picture slip from the bag and *save it.* If two players call out an answer at exactly the same moment, they may both pick a slip.

The caller begins each round by posing a new addition or subtraction problem. A round always ends when a player finds the answer on a plate and wins the right to pick a slip. The players save their slips in order to collect three of the same picture. A "wild card" slip may stand for any picture. If a player gives a *wrong* answer to an arithmetic problem, he must forfeit one of his slips (if he has any) to an opponent, who is chosen by lot to be the "picker." Without looking, the "picker" takes a slip from those collected by the player. The first player to collect three identical pictures or two identical ones plus a wild card wins the game (two wild cards plus a picture are not acceptable).

If all the players are over 8 or 9, you may include multiplication or division examples whose answers are 0 to 9. You may even include fractions and percentage problems, such as ¼ of 28, ½ of 18, or 10 percent of 40.

VARIATIONS

Easy variation (ages 4 and up)

Play the game exactly as above. However, instead of giving the children addition or subtraction problems, the leader asks any simple question with an answer from 0 to 9, such as "What number comes after 1, 2, 3, __?" Other questions might be the number of people in your family, fingers on one hand, shoes you are wearing, and so on.

Make a Hundred

Play in the same way as Turn Over Triplets, but instead of picture slips use thirty number slips: five slips with the number 2, five slips with the number 5, four slips with the number 10, four slips with the number 15, four slips with the number 20, four slips with the number 25, two slips with a −5, and two slips with a −10. You might include a sad face on the minus slips so they will not be confused with +5 or +10.

Each time a player is first to find a right answer on a license, he picks a number slip. The first player to collect slips which equal or exceed 100 wins the game. Again, if a player gets a wrong answer, his opponents choose for the right to pick one of his slips. The "picker" takes a slip without looking and adds the amount to his own score. I have found that children over eight or nine prefer this variation to the standard game.

Knock It Off!

(moderate to heavy traffic)

Number of players Even number (2, 4, or 6)

Suggested age 6 and up

Time 15 to 25 minutes

Object To knock off all the items on your opponent's list before he can knock off yours

Materials Felt pen and notebook for each player or team

Preparation Team One (low team) writes down the numbers from 0 to 4 and the letters from A to M on a notebook page. Here is the list Team One copies: 0, 1, 2, 3, 4, A, B, C, D, E, F, G, H, I, J, K, L, M.

Team Two (high team) writes down the numbers from 5 to 9 and the letters from N to Z. Here is the list Team Two copies: 5, 6, 7, 8, 9, N, O, P, Q, R, S, T, U, V, W, X, Y, Z.

Team One and Team Two now trade notebooks and the game is ready to begin.

Rules At the starting signal, each player (or team) must look at the passing license plates for the numbers and letters on his opponent's list so he can knock them off. Players cross the numbers and letters off the lists as they find them. Only one call can be made on any one license plate. The first player (or team) to knock off all the items on his opponent's list, wins the game.

VARIATION

This is a game which older children (ages 9 and up) will enjoy. In this variation, a player can knock off an opponent's letter or number only if it appears next to one of his own letters or numbers on the license plate. For example, if he spots a plate which reads, 8 2 1 A R Z, and he is on the low team, he may say, "My 2 knocks off your 8," or "My A knocks off your R." Then he crosses the number 8 (*or* the letter R) off his list of targets. On the other hand, if a high team player notices this plate first, he may say, "My 8 knocks off your 2," or "My R knocks off your A."

Note that for this variation letters knock off letters and numbers knock off numbers. A license plate can be used for only one hit. If both teams call a hit at the same moment, both may cross that target off their list. However, once a team has started to speak, the other may not interrupt until the first team has finished. Naturally, if either team makes a mistake in its call, the hit does not count.

The first team to wipe out its opponent's list wins the game. If both teams still have numbers and letters left at the end of 40 minutes of play, the team with the most "survivors" wins the game.

Note There is a blocking maneuver which either team can use to protect itself from attack. Let's say that a Team One player sees a license plate which reads, 3 6 7 P A T. He has already crossed T off his list, so he doesn't need to hit it. However, his A has not yet been captured and is vulnerable to attack. To save his A, he can say, "My A knocks off your T," so that his opponent can't hit him.

Dead End

(moderate traffic)

Suggested age 8 and up

Time 30 to 45 minutes

Object To form the greatest number of words on your highway chart without running into dead ends

Materials Notebook and felt pen for each player

Preparation Each player should draw a 5 × 5 square in his notebook (25 squares in all). He should put a small dot in the center square (the third square in the third row) to designate the starting position.

Rules Each player is assigned a car color. Choose common ones, such as blue, white, green, or yellow. The youngest player goes first and looks for a car of his color. When he spots one, he looks at the letters on the license plate and chooses any one he wishes. Let's say it's the letter Z. He calls out "Z," and everyone, including the caller, must write a Z in his center box (the box with the dot). Players should also write the number 1 in the corner of this box to show that it is their first move. Now the next player takes a turn. He looks for a car of his color and calls out any letter on that license. If no letter appeals to him, he may wait for a second car of his color. However, he must pick one of the letters on the second car, whether he likes them or not. All players write the next letter (let's say it's an A) one box away from the Z in any direction they wish—horizontally, vertically or diagonally (the starred boxes in the diagram)— and place a small number 2 in the corner of that box to designate it as their second move.

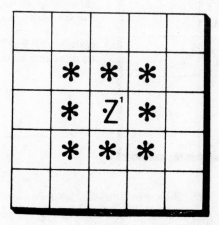

Now the third player (or the first, if you're playing a two-person game), takes a turn, looking for a car of his color and choosing one of the letters which appears on the license. All players write this new letter in any box adjacent to the one where they wrote the A. Along with the new letter, players write the next number, 3. Throughout the game, each letter called must be placed one box away in any direction from the previous letter. Players will want to place their letters strategically so that they begin to form words of two letters or more in a straight line, horizontally and vertically, forward or backward.

There may come a point in the game at which one of the players reaches a dead end. That is, in the course of his moves, he traps himself and cannot place a letter one box away from his previous one. At this point, the player writes "Dead End" at the top of his page and places the next letter in any box adjacent to one already written in. At the end of the game, the player will receive penalty points for each dead end he encountered. The illustration shows an instance in which a player reached a dead end (the numbers in the boxes show the order of his moves).

B^8	P^7	$*$		
E^6	R^3	A^2		
D^5	O^4	Z^1		

On his eighth move, this player forced himself into a dead end. He could have avoided it by placing B in the starred box. Instead, by trying to form a word, he trapped himself.

Players continue to take turns until all 25 spaces are filled in. Then they add up their scores on each line by counting the words they have formed horizontally and vertically, both forward and backward. Two-letter words score 2 points, three-letter words, 3 points, and so on. Players may count more than one word on a line, as long as each word contains at least one letter not found in the others. If one or more letters are repeated in two different words, they are scored in each word they appear in. When a player has totaled his score, he must subtract 5 points for each dead end. The player with the most points wins the game. See the illustration for a sample game which has been scored.

B [8]	P [7]	D [9]	I [10]	S [11]	IS (2) ID (2)
E [6]	R [3]	A [2]	N [14]	T [12]	ARE (3) RANT (4)
D [5]	O [4]	·Z [1]	E [15]	U [13]	DOZE (4)
E [25]	V [23]	E [21]	I [16]	N [17]	EVE (3) VEIN (4)
Q [24]	E [22]	I [20]	T [19]	E [18]	TIE (3)

BED **PROVE** **DAZE** **IN (2)** **STUN**
(3) **(5)** **(4)** **TIE (3)** **(4)**

Score: 46–5* = 41

*Dead End, 8th move

Adaptation for one player To play this game, the single player will need a bag of commercial letter tiles or 26 letter slips from A to Z. To begin, the player writes down a letter which appears on the plate of a car of his chosen color. On every other turn, he picks a letter from the bag and writes that letter in any box adjacent to the one he just wrote in. He should always put the letters he picked back into the bag. In all other respects, the game is the same as the standard version. When all 25 boxes are filled, he adds up his score as described above. The player may look at this rating scale to see how well he did and perhaps try to improve his score in another round.

Under 20: Weak
21 to 30: Fair
31 to 40: Good
40 to 50: Very good
46 or more: Excellent!

The Map Game

(an ongoing game played by all ages)

Whether you're riding near home or thousands of miles away, you're sure to pass travelers from every corner. Why not make a game of spotting them? Make a photocopy of this map for each member of your family, and paste one at the back of each person's notebook.

Any time your family is on the road and someone notices a plate from a new state or province he can color that state or province with a light-colored crayon or felt pen (yellow or pink is ideal). Only one person may claim any one plate. After three or four trips, your maps will start to become colorful. The first person to fill in his entire map should win some small treat.

Car Poker

(moderate to heavy traffic)

Suggested age   8 and up

Time   15 to 30 minutes

Object   To get the highest score by making the best poker hands

Materials   Notebook and crayon or felt pen for each player

Note   Refer to the following point values when playing:

One pair: two identical numbers or letters, 10 points
Two pair: two identical numbers and two identical letters, 20 points
Straight: three successive numbers or letters (456, 012, DEF, and so on), 25 points. The numbers or letters don't have to appear in the correct order on the license plate.

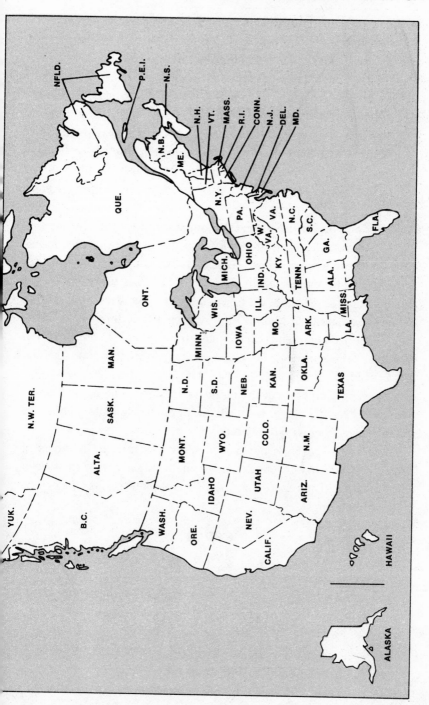

Three of a kind: Any three identical numbers or letters, 35
  points
Full house: three identical numbers and two identical letters *or*
  two identical numbers and three identical letters, 50 points
High number or letter: 5 points (counted only when *no* player
  has received a score)
Bonus score: If two or more players get a pair, a straight, or
  three of a kind, the one with the *highest* number or letter
  combination gets a 5-point bonus. This rule does not apply
  to two pair or full house

Rules Each player is assigned a common car color like blue, green,
white, brown, yellow, and red. Players will use one or two license
plates to make a poker hand. To begin round one, each player writes
down the plate number of the first car of his color which passes (he
should wait for a plate with five or more numbers and letters).
Players examine their "hands" to decide which letters and numbers
they want to keep and which ones they want to discard. For
example, let's suppose one player writes down the plate number
3 6 6 W H N. If he wants to keep the sixes and discard everything
else, he simply crosses out the numbers and letters he doesn't want:
3 6 6 W H N. If a player is satisfied with the whole plate number, he
doesn't have to cross out anything.

Players who do cross out one or more of the plate numbers or
letters write down the plate number of the next car of their color
which passes. They write down the second plate number below the
first one, like this:

3̸ 6 6 W̸ H̸ N̸

6 4 2 B X D

The player who wrote down this second plate number must cross
two figures off the second plate and keep the rest like this:

3̸ 6 6 W̸ H̸ N̸

6 4̸ 2̸ B X D

The player always keeps the same number of letters from the second plate as he crossed off the first one. The numbers and letters which have *not* been crossed out make up the player's final hand, in this case, 6 6 6 B X D. This lucky player ends up with three of a kind and receives a score of 35 points (if another player also gets three of a kind, the player with the higher hand gets 5 extra points. Numbers and letters are *not* compared to one another. Therefore, if one player gets M M M and another player gets 8 8 8, both players score 35 points. Players reveal their final hands to the other players, and all mark down a score for the first hand.

Play four more hands in the same manner, recording a score for each one. After five rounds of play, the person with the highest score wins the game.

Note If some young players are in the game, I suggest playing one or two trial hands, so that everyone gets the knack. Older children can help the younger ones with scoring if necessary.

Blast Off!

(moderate traffic)

Suggested age 9 and up

Time 15 to 30 minutes

Object To be the first pilot to "blast off" by circling all the letters in your countdown word

Materials Felt pen and notebook for each player

Preparation Each player must print a *different* word of exactly 10 letters at the top of his notebook page (capitals and plurals are permitted). Here are some choices (you can supply others):

Television	Admiration	Handlebars	Presenting
California	Benevolent	Stationery	Reconsider
Washington	Everything	Revolution	Collection

The example here is blackboard. Above each of the letters the player writes the numbers from 1 to 10 consecutively.

1	2	3	4	5	6	7	8	9	10
B	L	A	C	K	B	O	A	R	D

Rules A player must circle all the letters in his word before he can blast off. Let's see how a player accomplishes this, and then we can fit the procedure into the game.

To begin, Player One looks at all the passing license plates until he finds one which has one of the letters in his word, "blackboard." Perhaps he spots a license with the letter C. Since the word "blackboard" contains a C, he looks in his notebook at the number written above that letter. He finds it is 4, so he calls out "C—4" and crosses out the letter C by drawing a diagonal line through it.

The other players in the car must now try to find a license plate which has the number 4 *before* Player One can find another letter in his word. If one of his opponents does spot a 4 and calls it out, Player One loses his C and must rewrite the letter right below the first one:

1	2	3	4	5	6	7	8	9	10
B	L	A	¢	K	B	O	A	R	D
			C						

However, if Player One calls out another letter in his word (perhaps "L—2") before his opponents can find a 4, his first letter is *safe,* and he may circle it:

1	2	3	4	5	6	7	8	9	10
B	L	A	Ⓒ	K	B	O	A	R	D

Of course, the second letter he has crossed out, the L, is now in danger. If any opponent finds and calls out the number 2 before Player One finds a third letter in his word, another L must be written below the first one. But if Player One does find a third letter before a 2 is called out, he may circle the letter L. (The third letter is now in jeopardy.) Whenever a letter is rewritten, Player One must search for it all over again. There is no limit to the number of times a letter may be rewritten. You'll see, however, that it doesn't happen often. Note that no matter how many times a letter is crossed out, you circle the top one when you win a letter.

In the sample word "blackboard" there are two B's and two A's. If Player One spots either of these letters on a license, he has the choice of calling "B—1" or "B—6" or "A—3" or "A—7." The number he chooses to call will depend on the numbers on the licenses he sees around him. For example, if he sees a nearby license with the number 1, he is better off calling out "B—6." Of course, if B—6 has already been circled, he has no choice but to say "B—1" and hope that his opponents don't notice a license with a 1.

Note that for this game the number 10 consists of a 1 immediately followed by a zero, not by the letter O. If Player One calls "D-10," his opponent must find a license with this sequence of numbers in order to cancel the D.

Eventually, Player One circles 9 out of his 10 letters. Finally he spots a license with the letter K and calls out "K—5." As his opponents are looking for a license with a 5, Player One begins *counting down* out loud at a moderate pace, "10—9—8—7—6—5—4—" etc. If any opponent interrupts the countdown by finding and calling out the number 5, Player One must rewrite the K and find another. Otherwise, Player One may finish off the countdown, "–3–2–1, BLAST OFF!" The first player to blast off wins the game.

Now let's put all this into the context of the game.

All the players, of course, are looking for the letters in their own words at the same time, so that everyone has to concentrate on two things at once. On the one hand, the players are looking for the letters in their own words, and on the other, they are trying to spot and call out the last number their opponent called in order to stop his progress. Since it's pretty tough to do both things at once (especially when there are more than two players), the game moves at a fast pace. A player may play offensively (looking for his own letters) or defensively (concentrating more on his opponent's numbers). Some sharp-eyed youngsters (or adults) can do both at the same time.

After the first player blasts off, the others may continue to play for second place, third place, and so on.

Night Lights

*(moderate traffic on 3-lane highways,
although it will work on 2 lanes)*

Number of players Even number (2, 4, or 6)

Suggested age 6 and up (or younger, if the child knows right from left)

Time 10 to 20 minutes

Object To be the first player or team to find and call out 10 directional signal lights of the correct type ("righties" or "lefties")

Rules There may be times when your family is on the road at night and finds it impossible to play any of the other highway observation games in this chapter. Night Lights is perfect for such occasions.

Divide the players into two equal teams. One team will be the righties and the other the lefties.

Notes (If one of the players is right-handed and the other is left-handed, it makes sense to have them look for cars with the corresponding signal. However, if both players write with the same hand, allow the younger child to look for signals which correspond to the hand he writes with.)

At the starting signal the righties look for and call out cars that have on their right blinker lights, while the lefties look for cars that have on their left blinker lights. You're sure to spot many of both types when cars change lanes or enter or exit the road you are driving on. Keep score out loud as you go along. The first team to find 10 of the correct type of signal wins the game.

If a child (or team) calls out the wrong signal ("right" for a left blinker or vice versa), the opposing child or team automatically scores an extra point.

Adaptation for one player The single player should have a set time limit (15 minutes is just about right) to find as many right (or left) signals as he can. He should keep score for himself out loud. When he gets home, he may enjoy looking at this rating scale to see how well he fared:

Under 7: Poor sense of direction
8 to 11: You're in the right direction
12 to 17: You're blinking better than average
18 or over: Directional expert!

If your gang finds highway observation games the most fun of all, you'll find a number of others to enjoy in Chapter 4 (Out Loud Games) and Chapter 7 (Backseat Board Games). Or, if you prefer a break from road watching, try some of the pen and paper games which follow!

Materials
1. Felt pen or crayon for each player
2. Spiral notebook for each player
3. Watch with a second hand (for most games, you can use a one- or two-minute egg timer
4. Paper bag
5. Pair of dice in a clear glass jar (in most cases, you can use a standard spinner, numbered 1–6, or a deck of playing cards instead of dice)

Optional Materials

1. Bag of commercial letter tiles
2. Play money
3. Commercial follow-the-dots picture for each player (pictures should have the same number of dots)
4. About 30 drinking straws and cup or container to put them in
5. Pocket dictionary for word games

PEN AND PAPER

3·PPG

GAMES

There's a lot of easy fun in this chapter—word and number games, memory quizzes, games of strategy, and even some geography. Most of the games require nothing more than a felt pen and paper, although a pocket dictionary is helpful for word games. All can be enjoyed by the whole family.

Crossword Contest

Number of players 2 or more (unless instructions indicate otherwise, all games in this chapter require 2 or more players)

Suggested age 7 and up

Time 15 to 25 minutes

Object To make as many words as possible, vertically and horizontally

Materials Notebook and crayon or felt pen for each player

Preparation Each player draws in his notebook a box with 25 squares—five across and five down

Rules Each player draws a blank 5 × 5 square. The first player calls out any letter of the alphabet he wishes. All players (including the caller) write that letter in any one of the 25 boxes. Then the second player calls a letter, and everyone writes that letter in any one of the 24 empty boxes. When all players have had a turn to call a letter, start again with the first player. Players continue calling letters until all 25 boxes are filled (letters can be repeated as often as players want). Since the object of the game is to make as many words as possible, players should call letters carefully and place them to form words when they can. Horizontal words must be written left to right and vertical words, top to bottom.

When the game is over, players add their scores by counting up words. A word must contain at least three letters (for seven- and eight-year-olds you can count two-letter words), and only *one* word may be counted on each line. Proper nouns, slang, and abbreviations are not counted. Three-letter words score 3 points, four-letter words, 4 points, and five-letter words, 5 points. Write the number of points scored for each line next to that line. Add the scores for all horizontal and vertical rows to arrive at your total (see sample square). The player with the highest score wins. Fifty is a perfect score and nearly impossible to get.

Adaptation for one player Write the 26 letters of the alphabet on separate index cards or slips of paper and place them in a paper bag. (If you have letter tiles, use those instead.) Draw a 5 × 5 square on a page of your notebook. Play the game as described above. On alternate turns, you may write any letter you want in one of the 25 boxes. However, every other turn you must pick a letter from the bag and write the letter you picked in a box. After you pick a letter,

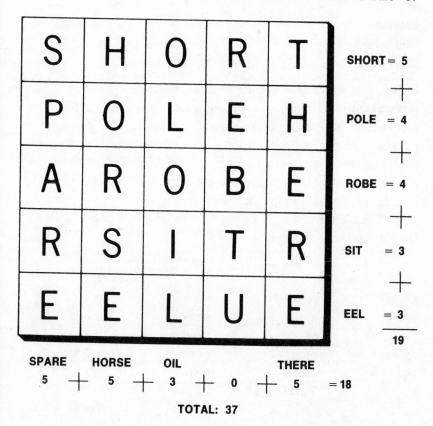

put it back in the bag. When all the boxes are filled, add up your score. How close did you come to a perfect score of 50? Try again and see if you can come closer.

Word Detective

Number of players one or more

Suggested age 8 and up

Time 10 to 20 minutes

Object To spell as many words as you can from the letters in one long word

Materials Notebook and felt pen for each player

Rules Players write the same word of ten letters or more at the top of their pages—for instance, "grandfather," "understanding," "refrigeration." They have a set time limit (perhaps 15 minutes) to write down as many words of three or more letters as they can from the letters in the long word. (See sample game.) Proper nouns, abbreviations, and slang words are not permitted. At the end of the time limit, players add up their scores. Three-letter words score 3 points, four-letter words, 4 points, and so on. The player with the highest total wins the game.

Sample Word: **Preparation**

Player A		**Player B**	
tire = 4	rate = 4	tin = 3	nip = 3
tear = 4	eat = 3	nap = 3	rare = 4
paper = 5	tea = 3	paint = 5	tear = 4
rape = 4	pear = 4	part = 4	eat = 3
tape = 4	apart = 5	pear = 4	ear = 3
tip = 3	**Total = 43**	pain = 4	earn = 4
		tip = 3	**Total = 47**

Children of eight or younger should be permitted to use two-letter words. If the younger child is still at a disadvantage (for example, if he is competing with an adult), he should be spotted some points to make the game fairer.

You're on TV!

Suggested age 7 and up

Time 15 to 30 minutes, depending on the number of rounds

Object To earn the highest score by giving more correct answers than other game show contestants

Materials Notebook and felt pen for each player, watch with second hand or two-minute egg timer

Rules Players draw large TV screens on their pages, covering most of the page. An adult names a category which players write at the top of their screens. Choose a category that all players can handle. Some suggestions:

States of the United States

Presidents of the United States

Four-legged animals

Fruits

Vegetables

Breeds of dogs

Movie and television stars

Countries of the world

Colors

Rocks, minerals, and precious stones

Things that fly

Toys and games

Cartoon characters

Beverages

Furniture

Song titles

Types of jobs

Kinds of stores

Candy bars

Articles of clothing

Flowers

Birds

Fish or other sea creatures

Parts of the body

Sports

Fairy tales

Nursery rhymes

Ice cream flavors

Types of transportation

Instruments

Girls' names

Boys' names

Names of dances

Things that are green (or any specific color)

You can also use word categories:

Words which begin with a consonant combination (br, bl, ch, cr, and so on)

Words which end with a specific letter combination (st, nd, nk, tion)

Words which begin and end with the same letter

Words with double letters

Homonyms (words which sound alike but are spelled differently, such as sail and sale)

I purposely mentioned enough categories here so that you can refer to this list whenever you need ideas for any category game.

Players have two minutes (or five minutes, if you prefer) to think of as many words as possible which fit the chosen category. When the time is called, each player reads his list. He scores 2 points for responses which *no* other player has thought of and one point for responses that appear on other screens. Spelling doesn't count, except in the case of word categories. Play four more rounds with a new category each time. At the end of five rounds, the player with the highest score is the champion.

To make the contest more even, younger children should be spotted a few points.

VARIATIONS

Someone who is not participating in the game (the driver, for instance) thinks of a secret word which fits the chosen category. For example, if the category is "musical instruments," the secret word might be "harp." At the end of a round, the secret word is revealed. Anyone who has that word on his list may add an extra 5 points to his score.

To make the game feel like a television show, give each child a chance to be the master of ceremonies. He can even use an empty paper towel or toilet paper roll as a "microphone." Players may enjoy making up silly commercials between rounds.

Adaptation for one player Play three rounds, using an egg timer so you can keep time for yourself. Record the total of your three scores. Now try three new categories to see whether you can improve your score.

The Memory Game

Suggested age 7 and up

Time 15 to 30 minutes

Object To remember more items on your opponent's list than he remembers on yours

Materials Notebook and felt pen for each player

Preparation Players make lists of 15 to 20 unrelated objects (all lists should have the same number of items). Here is a sample list:

Ball	Book	Penny	Marble
Key	Cookie	Radio	Flower
Door	Rubber band	Toothbrush	Milk
Hat	Towel	Refrigerator	Shoe
Pencil	Rattle	Balloon	Spider

Rules Choose one player to be "it." He shows his list to the others. Everyone has one minute to study it. At the end of a minute, the player puts his list away and everyone (including the player who made the list) has five minutes to write down as many of the items as he can remember. When time is called, players read their lists and score one point for every correct item. Now a different player becomes "it" and shows his list to everyone. When all players have had a turn to be "it," they add up their points. The player with the highest total wins the game.

With younger children, the list can have 10 items instead of 15 or 20. If children can't read, they can make a simple picture list instead of a word list.

Adaptation for one player In advance, an adult makes up two different picture or word lists, each with 10 to 20 items. The child studies the first list for one minute, puts it away, and writes down or recites as many items as he can remember in five minutes. He plays again with the second list. Can he better his score?

VARIATIONS

What's in the Box? (ages 7 and up)

Fill a shoebox or shopping bag with 15 to 20 items gathered from the car or from supplies on hand. Some good choices might be:

Road map   Egg timer or watch
Pocket comb   Paper or plastic cup
Lipstick   Tissue or napkin
Keys   Plastic spoon or fork
Bobby pin   Gum or candy wrapper
Playing card   Penny or other coin
Felt pen or crayon   Nail file
Shoelace

Players are given a few minutes to study the contents of the box or bag. Then it is put away. Players have five or 10 minutes to write down as many articles as they can remember. When time is up, the contents of the box or bag are revealed again. The player who remembered the most items wins the game (a single player can simply try to come as close a possible to a perfect score).

Now You See It, Now You Don't (ages 5 and up)

Put about 15 small objects found in the car into a shoebox, shopping bag, or other container (see the list above for ideas).

Everyone has a minute or two to study the contents of the box or bag. The first player up removes one object while the others look away or hide their eyes. When he says "ready," the other players look in the box or bag and try to guess which object was taken away. The first player to call out the missing object scores one point. If no one guesses it in one minute, the person who removed the object gets the point. Each player gets five turns to be up. When all players have had their turns, the one with the highest point score wins the game. You can also try these variations with the contents of a purse or glove compartment.

Triangle Dot Game

Suggested age 4 and up

Time 10 to 20 minutes

Object To capture the most triangles

Materials Notebook and crayon or felt pen for each player

Preparation Draw this triangular arrangement in one player's notebook:

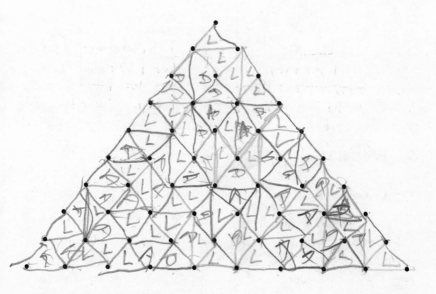

The first row has one dot, the last, ten. Each successive row has one more dot than the row before it.

Rules The first player connects any two dots with a straight line. Each player in turn does the same. Whenever a player's line completes a triangle, he puts his initials in it and takes another turn. When all dots have been connected, players count up their triangles. The one who has the most wins the game.

VARIATIONS

Square Dot Game (ages 4 and up)

Draw a 10 × 10 dot diagram. Connect the dots to form boxes.

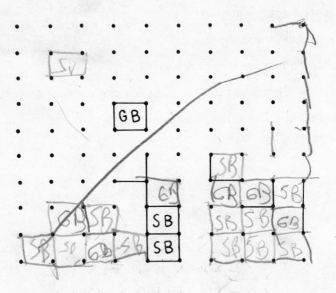

Number Dot Game (ages 7 and up)

Randomly substitute the numbers 1 through 9 for dots.

2	1	3	5	4	2	6	1	4	2
5	2	1	3	4	7	2	3	1	6
7	3	2	1	6	4	5	2	2	5
4	1	1	2	3	3	6	5	7	5
6	3	2	8	1	1	7	1	4	4
4	2	2	1	3	3	3	6	5	7
3	3	4	2	2	5	5	7	1	1
9	1	7	2	4	3	5	1	8	3
2	7	1	3	4	2	8	6	1	9
1	3	2	4	3	5	4	6	5	7

For younger players, use only the numbers from 1 to 5. The first player connects any two numbers with a horizontal or vertical line. Before he does so, however, he must tell the sum of the two numbers he wants to connect (for example, if he draws a line between a 1 and a 3, he must say "4"). If he says the *wrong* sum, he loses that turn. To make a box, a player must give the sum of *all four numbers* which make up the box. If he can't, he loses his turn, and the next player gets to try for the box. When all the boxes have been formed, the player who has captured the most wins the game.

Five in a Line

Number of Players 2

Suggested age 4 and up

Time 5 to 30 minutes

Object To be the first player to get five marks in a line

Materials Notebook and felt pen for each player

Preparation Draw a 10 × 10 square

Rules One player chooses X's and the other O's. Players alternate writing their symbols in any of the boxes. The first player to get five in a line in any direction (horizontally, vertically, or diagonally) wins the game.

If You Lose, You Win!

Number of players 2

Suggested age 3 and up

Object To *avoid* being the player to put an X in the last box along the path

Materials Felt pen for each player and one notebook

Preparation Draw a winding path with 20 spaces or more, as shown here.

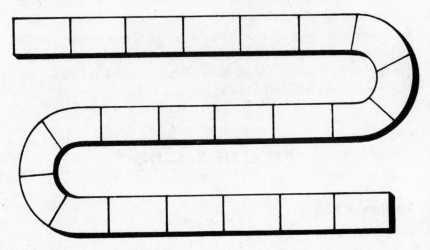

Rules Starting with the first box, the first player draws an X in one, two, or three consecutive boxes along the path. The next player does the same, beginning with the next blank box. Players take turns drawing one, two, or three X's until they reach the end of the path. The player who is forced to put an X in the *last* box along the path loses the game. Play five rounds (the paths are easy to make). The player who wins the most rounds is the champ.

Category Letter Quiz

Suggested age 7 and up

Time 15 to 25 minutes

Object To think of a correct word for each letter and category

Materials Notebook and felt pen for each player

Preparation Think of a five-letter word with five different letters, such as "plant." Players draw a 6 × 6 square (36 boxes in all) as shown and block out the box in the upper left-hand corner. They write the chosen five-letter word across the top row. Then they choose five categories and write one in each of the five boxes in the first vertical column. (See the game You're on TV!, page 69 in this chapter, for category ideas.)

	P	L	A	N	T
metal things	pot	ladder	ankle bracelet		tin can
fruits	plum	lemon	apple	nectarine	tangerine
insects and spiders	praying mantis	ladybug	ant		tarantula
dogs	poodle	Labrador retriever	Alaskan husky		terrier
living room furniture	piano	lamp			television

Rules At the starting signal, players have 10 minutes to think of words for each category which begin with the letters at the head of the columns (you can also play 15-minute rounds). For example, in the sample game the player was able to think of a fruit which began with P, L, A, N, and T. The other categories gave him a little more trouble. When time is up, everyone adds up his score, counting one point for each correct response. High score wins.

VARIATIONS

1. For a longer game, draw a 9 × 9 square (81 boxes), blanking out the box in the upper left-hand corner. Across the top row write an eight-letter word with no repeated letters. (Some examples are "children," "sprouted," "sandwich," "thousand," and "reaction.") Write eight different categories in the first vertical row. Play this longer version with a 20-minute time limit.

2. Players write the letters from A to Z on a page of notebook paper, leaving a whole line after each letter. They choose *one* category (perhaps, Animals), and everyone writes it as a title at the top of his page. At the starting signal, players have 20 minutes to think of words for every letter of the alphabet which fit the chosen category. It's perfectly all right—as a matter of fact, desirable—for players to write *more* than one response for each letter if they are able to. When time is called, players count one point for every correct response, and minus one point for every letter with *no* response or with an incorrect one. High score wins.

Adaptation for one player Choose the version of the category letter quiz that you like the best. Play the game *twice* using different categories each time. Can you better your own score?

Jumbled Words

Suggested age 8 and up

Time 10 to 15 minutes

Object To unscramble your opponent's list of jumbled words before he can unscramble yours

Materials Notebook and felt pen for each player

Preparation Each player makes up a list of 10 five-letter words, scrambling up the order of the letters—for example P A Y P H (happy) T R A T S (start).

Rules Players fold their jumbled word lists in half, so the writing doesn't show, and hand them to an opponent. (If three people are playing, Player A gives his list to Player B, Player B to Player C, and

Player C to Player A.) At the starting signal, players open up their lists. They try to unscramble the words and write the correctly spelled word next to the jumbled one. The first player to finish his list yells out, "Done." The other players turn their papers over while the "Winner" reads his list. If all of his words are correct, he wins the game. The other players continue to play for second place, third place, and so on. However, if the first player made mistakes, play is resumed as before. The false "winner" gets a 30-second penalty before he can work on his list again.

Sometimes it is possible to make two or more different words with the same five letters. For example, "teams," "steam," "mates," and "meats" all have the same letters. As long as the player has successfully unscrambled the letters to form a correct English word, his answer is valid, even if it isn't the word the opposing player had in mind. If no player is able to unscramble all his words at the end of 15 minutes, the one who has the most correct answers wins the game. If a player can't unscramble a word because his opponent didn't include the right letters, his opponent loses one point for each error.

Note If this game is too difficult for your group, use three- or four-letter words. If it's too easy, use six- or seven-letter words.

Adaptation for one player In advance, make up two scrambled word lists for your child. He tries to unscramble the words on the first list as quickly as he can and records the time it took him to finish. If he has not completed the list in 15 minutes, he stops anyway and scores one point for each correct response. Then he tries the second list. Can he complete it faster than the first?

Letter Tic-Tac-Toe

Number of players 2

Suggested age 7 and up

Time 10 to 25 minutes

Object To capture three letters in a line by thinking of the most words that begin with that letter

Materials Different color crayon (or felt pen) for each player, one notebook and watch with second hand

Preparation Draw a tic-tac-toe board, and write a letter of the alphabet in each square.

```
S | H | D
---------
M | B | F
---------
T | R | L
```

Rules The two players choose to see who goes first. The first player chooses any letter he wishes from the tic-tac-toe board and says a word that begins with that letter. Then the other player has 30 seconds (one minute for younger players) to say another word which begins with the same letter. Players alternate in this way until one of them can't think of another word that begins with that letter within the time limit. The player who gives the last successful answer gets to put a circle around the letter with his color crayon and to choose the next letter to play. As in tic-tac-toe, the first player to circle three letters in a row in any direction wins the game.

VARIATION

For a more difficult game, use a two-letter combination (such as ch, fl, wh, gl, sp, th, dr, pl, and bl). Players must say words which begin with the two letters. In all other respects, the game is the same.

Adaptation for one player For this version you need a pair of dice and a one-minute egg timer. The player chooses one box he would like to try for. He shoots the dice and has one minute to name as many words as he can that begin with that letter (or two-letter combination). He can keep count of his words with his fingers. At the end of one minute, if the player gives *more* responses than the number that appears on the dice, he captures that letter on the tic-tac-toe board and circles it. However, if he gives the same number or less than the number on the dice, his Phantom opponent wins the box. (Put a black X on letters that the Phantom captures.) Who will get tic-tac-toe—you or the Phantom?

Map Capture

Number of players   3 or more

Suggested age   9 and up

Time   30 to 45 minutes

Object   To capture the most states and provinces by correctly naming the surrounding states and provinces

Materials   Watch with second hand or egg timer, map (see page 57), notebook, and felt pen for each player

Rules   Players are given five minutes to study the map (you can take a shorter time if the players are geography buffs). One of the players is then chosen to be the first caller. The caller holds the map in such a way that the other players can't see it, names one state or province, and tells the number of states or provinces that border it.   For example, the caller may say, "Nevada—5." The other players have one minute to write down the names of the five states which border Nevada. If they aren't sure players should guess; however, they can't write down *more* than the total number of bordering states. At the end of one minute, the caller reads off the correct states. The player with the most correct answers captures that state and writes his name and the state on the "winner's sheet."

In case of a tie, the tied players can flip a coin or choose for the state.

Each player serves as caller for four rounds, naming a different state or province every round. When all players have had a turn to be caller for four rounds, the player who has captured the most states and provinces wins the game.

For a shorter game, give each caller fewer turns (either 1, 2, or 3). For a longer game, give each caller 5 or more turns.

Adaptation for two players An adult who is not playing makes up seven slips with the names of different states or provinces plus the number of states or provinces which border them. Put all the slips into a paper bag. The two players take a few minutes to study a map. Then one of the players picks a slip and both have one minute to write the names of the bordering states or provinces. When time is called, the player with the most correct answers captures that state or province. Play continues until no slips are left in the bag. The player who captures the most states or provinces wins the game.

Beram's Special Hangman

Number of players 2

Suggested age 7 and up

Time 20 to 45 minutes

Object To "hang" an entire figure before your opponent can guess your secret word

Materials Notebook and felt pen for each player

Rules The first player up is the "hangman." He thinks of a secret word and draws a dash for each letter in it. Alongside that, he draws a scaffold. His opponent must now try to guess the letters in the secret word. If he guesses a letter correctly, the hangman writes it on each dash where it belongs in the word. For example, if the secret word is "airplane" and the opponent guesses A, the hangman fills in the two A's in their proper places.

Each time the player makes a *wrong* guess, the hangman draws one part of the body on the scaffold in the following order: head, eyes (both drawn for one error), nose, mouth, hair, body, one arm, other arm, one leg, other leg (10 parts in all). Each time he guesses right, however, the hangman adds the new letter to the dashes (the player should write the letters he guesses at the top of his page so he won't try to guess them again by mistake). If the hangman is able to complete the figure before the player guesses the word, the round is over, and the hangman gets 15 points. If the player guesses the word before the figure is completed, the hangman gets one point for each body part he has drawn on the hanging post.

At the end of the round, the players switch roles. The guesser becomes the hangman and the hangman becomes the guesser. As in the other round, the new hangman makes up a secret word of the *same length* as the first. The round is played in the same way. The player with the highest score wins the game.

For a longer, more exciting game, each player should have two or three turns as hangman.

Sandwich Cookies

Suggested age   8 and up

Time   30 minutes

Object   To earn the most points by forming words ("sandwich cookies") with the required first and last letters

Materials   Notebook and felt pen for each player, one letter-value sheet for each player (optional)

Preparation   Each player should jot down or refer to the following letter values:

A—1	H—2	O—1	V—4
B—2	I—1	P—4	W—3
C—3	J—4	Q—5	X—5
D—2	K—5	R—2	Y—5
E—1	L—2	S—2	Z—5
F—4	M—4	T—2	
G—3	N—3	U—1	

Rules   Choose any word of 10 letters or more, such as "grandmother," "blackboard," "stagecoach," or "flashlight." Players write the chosen word in a vertical column on the left side of the page, as shown in the sample game. On the right side of the page, they write the word backward in a vertical column. Draw lines joining each letter in the first column with each letter in the second column. At the starting signal, players write a word on each line that begins and ends with the letters on that line. The words can be any length, though the longer the words, the more points they are worth. Players should try to use letters with the highest point values. They have 20 minutes to work on their sheets (the timekeeper should warn players when there are only five minutes left). Proper nouns, abbreviations, and slang words are not permitted. When time is called, players use their letter value sheets to add up their scores. The player with the highest score wins the game.

				Score
G	grandfather	**R**		23
R	revenue	**E**		13
A	arch	**H**		8
N	nourishment	**T**		22
D	do	**O**		3
M	mom	**M**		9
O	ordered	**D**		11
T	transportation	**N**		27
H	hernia	**A**		10
E	entertainer	**R**		19
R	requiring	**G**		19

Total: 164

If younger children are playing with older ones, spot them from 10 to 50 points to give them an advantage.

Adaptation for one player Try this game twice, using words of equal length for each round. Can you better your own score?

Find the Tens

Suggested age 7 and up

Time 25 minutes

Object To find and circle the most number combinations which add up to 10

Materials Notebook and felt pen for each player

Preparation Draw the following 10 X 10 square in each player's notebook (you can write the digits in any sequence you want, as long as each player has the same numbers in the same places)

4	8	3	7	6	2	4	7	5	1
1	8	2	4	5	5	1	7	6	4
9	2	5	7	3	8	8	2	3	6
5	1	2	4	4	6	5	4	9	1
7	6	1	8	3	2	1	4	3	6
3	2	8	5	7	9	4	3	7	2
8	6	4	3	7	1	9	4	2	1
2	4	6	2	1	5	7	5	5	6
6	9	8	2	1	7	2	3	3	9
4	3	2	9	7	3	6	5	7	8

Rules At the starting signal, players have 20 minutes to circle as many number combinations as they can which add up to 10. The combinations can have any number of digits, but must be found in one straight line—horizontally, vertically, or diagonally. Some combinations may overlap as shown. At the end of the time limit, the player who has circled the most correct combinations wins the game.

With younger children, you may want to use only numbers from 1 to 5 and use 6 instead of 10 as the total to search for.

VARIATIONS

1. Using the same square, choose another sum which the children must circle (numbers from 10 to 20 work best). For example, your new game might be called, "Find the Twelves."

2. Make only one copy of the square. The players take turns circling number combinations which equal 10. If a player can't find a combination within a time limit of two minutes, he is eliminated from the game. The remaining players continue circling combinations until only one player is left. He is the winner.

Adaptation for one player This game easily lends itself to single play. Give the player a copy of the number square to circle combinations which add up to 10. When he has found as many as he can within 20 minutes, he rates himself:

> 10–20 combinations: Fair
> 20–30 combinations: Good
> 31–40 combinations: Very good
> 41–50 combinations: Excellent
> Over 50: Expert!

How Well Do You Know Each Other?

Suggested age 8 and up

Time 30 to 60 minutes

Object To score the most points by correctly predicting how other players will respond to the questions you ask them

Materials Notebook and felt pen for each player

Preparation Each player writes a list of 10 multiple-choice questions to find out the preferences of the other players. Here are a few sample questions:

Which of these colors do you like best?
red   yellow   blue   green

If you found $10 on the street, would you. . .
save it?   buy a toy?   buy ice cream for friends?   give it to a policeman?

When you stay up late, would you rather. . .
take a bath?   read?   watch TV?   play a game?

Each question should offer four choices. You can use any question which involves personal preferences. The questions can include your favorite place, the musical instrument you'd like to play, your favorite television show, the chore that you'd pick over others, the animal you'd like as a pet, the sport you'd like to play, the age you'd like to be, your favorite type of jewelry, your favorite means of transportation, or your *least* favorite of any of the above.

Rules The first player reads his questions aloud—one question at a time. He should read the choices two times. Each of the other players writes down his preference. When the questioner has gone through his whole list, he turns to one player at a time and, looking at his list of questions, tries to guess that player's responses. The questioner receives 5 points for each correct prediction.

The next player now asks the questions on his list. It doesn't matter if a few of his questions are similar to those of the first player, since the four choices he offers are bound to be a little different. When all players have had a chance to ask their questions and predict the others' responses, the player with the highest score wins.

Notes At first, writing good multiple-choice questions may not be easy for children. However, once they've practiced, you'll be surprised how inventive their questions become!

For this game one strict rule should be: no poking fun at a player for the choices he picks. If kids suspect they're going to be teased, they won't give honest answers.

When you've had your fill of pen and paper games, you might enjoy trying the out loud games in Chapter 4.

Materials

1. Spiral notebook for each player
2. Felt pen or crayon for each player
3. Watch with a second hand or a one or two-minute egg timer
4. Shoebox, shopping bag, or other container

Optional Materials

1. Pocket dictionary for word games
2. Paper bag and dice in a glass jar for single player

OUT LOUD

4·OLG

GAMES

The games in this chapter could be called "no muss, no fuss." They require little or no preparation and few, if any, materials. There are games that allow for physical activity when your children are restless and storytelling games that will let them exercise their imaginations. They're perfect for spur-of-the-moment trips or for days when you're looking for quick and easy fun.

Sign-Language Questions

Suggested age   5 and up

Time   15 to 25 minutes

Object   To make the proper hand signals in response to category words

Materials   Felt pen and paper to keep score

Note   This game was invented by my son, Glen, when he was seven.

Rules   Before beginning the game, the players invent three hand signals or motions which stand for three general categories: animals, colors, and people's names. For example, *animal,* spin one finger around in a circular motion; *color,* open and close your two hands; and *person's name,* wiggle all 10 fingers.

Other signals might be clapping your hands twice, sticking out your tongue, snapping your fingers, slapping your knees, putting your hands on your head, and so on. Of course, the more alike the motions are, the more difficult the game will be. Children should practice the signals before they begin the game.

A player is chosen to be the first caller. He calls out words that fit one of the three general categories to one other player—for example, "tiger," "yellow," "Susan," "red," and so on. The person who receives the word must immediately respond to it with the proper hand signal indicating the correct category (once a player begins a signal, he cannot change it). If his signal is correct, he scores one point and continues "receiving" words. If he misses, either by giving the *wrong* hand signal or by hesitating for more than five seconds, his turn is over, and he records his score for the round. The caller turns to the next player and names category words for him until he misses a signal. When everyone has had a turn *except* the caller, another player takes over and calls words for him. The round is over when every player has recorded a score.

Play two more rounds in the same manner, giving a different person a chance to call each round. At the end of three rounds, players add up their three scores. Highest score wins.

VARIATIONS

1. For variety you may want to change the categories you use (see You're on TV!, page 69). Choose very general categories so the caller can think of words easily (he may repeat words if he has to).

2. Just as categories can be changed, so can the hand signals. When the kids give the right response *too* quickly, it's time for a change.

3. With children six and under or kids who are learning the game, you can start out with only *two* categories and two different hand motions. With children nine and over, you may want to graduate to four categories.

4. For a change of pace, you might enjoy reversing the steps of the game. In other words, the caller makes the hand motion and the player responds with a word that fits the category. For example, if the caller wiggled his fingers, the player might shout out "Jimmy."

One Step Ahead of the Game

Number of players   3 or more

Suggested age   5 and up

Time   10 to 20 minutes

Object   To copy the motions made by the leader, one step behind him

Rules   One child is chosen to be the first leader. That child makes one motion three times in a row—for example, clapping his hands three times. Then he immediately begins to make a *new* motion, such as patting his head three times. When the leader begins the second motion (patting his head), the rest of the players must begin making the first motion (clapping their hands three times). As the leader starts a third motion (perhaps, snapping his fingers three times), the other players are starting the second motion (patting their heads). In other words, the leader is always *one step ahead* of the other players. He invents new motions, repeats them three times, and the others copy him, one sequence behind. When a player makes a mistake, he receives one penalty point. When the leader fouls up, he gets a penalty point, too. No matter who makes the mistake, a new player becomes the leader for the next round. (Players take turns being leader throughout the game.) When a player has received 5 penalty points, he's out of the game. He becomes the leader for the rest of the game but no longer counts a score for himself. The remaining players are eliminated as they accumulate 5 penalty points. The last player left wins the game.

VARIATION

For a tougher game, have each player copy the motions of the preceding player in a line. Thus, Player A makes a motion three times and Player B alone copies him as Player A starts his second motion. When Player B moves on to the second motion, player C begins the first, and so on. In other words, no two players are making the same motion at the same time (similar to a round-type song, with motions). Although Player A (the leader) gives the cue, each player (except Player A) has his own leader. In all other respects, the game is the same.

Notes   Sign-Language Questions and One Step Ahead of the Game are excellent games for increasing your children's power of concentration. As your kids get good at them, the leader can go through his motions (or category words) a little faster. For a greater challenge, try repeating each motion once or twice instead of three times. It's much harder!

These games are also great to play when kids begin to get restless from sitting in one place too long, since they allow some movement and release of excess energy.

Beram's Special Ghost

Suggested age   7 and up

Time   15 to 30 minutes

Object   To be the first player to spell the word "ghost"

Rules The first player calls out any letter he wishes from A to Z. Let's say he says "R." The next player now says another letter which he may place either *before* the R or after it—in other words, he can say "AR" or "RA." The next player adds a third letter either to the beginning of the two letters or to the end of them. The letter which he adds should lead to the formation of a word of three letters or more. However, he must be careful not to add a letter which *completes* a word, because if he does complete one, the player who went before him gets the first G of "ghost." The following are two sample rounds with two possible outcomes.

Sample A

Player 1: L
Player 2: **O**L
Player 3: **G**OL
Player 1: GOL**D**

Comments By adding a D, Player 1 completed the four-letter word GOLD, and thus Player 3, who went before him, gets a G.

Sample B

Player 1: N
Player 2: **N**O
Player 3: **A**NO
Player 1: **C**ANO
Player 2: CANO**E**

Player 1 receives a G for this round, since Player 2 completed the word "canoe." Note that in his first time up, Player 2 completed the word "no." However, he is *not* out since a word must have three or more letters to be counted as a game word.

Let's say that after Player 1 says "CANO," Player 2 can't think of a word which contains that sequence of letters. If he wants to, he can challenge Player 1 and ask him what word he had in mind. If Player 1 can't supply a word (because he has been bluffing), Player 2 gets the G instead. Slang words, proper nouns, and abbreviations are not permitted.

When a player gets a G, the player who completed the word begins a *new* word by saying another letter. As before, whenever a player completes a word, the player who went *before* him wins the next letter in the word "ghost" (perhaps, GH). Of course, if a player is challenged successfully on an incomplete word, the one who challenged him gets the letter instead. The first player to win all the letters in the word "ghost" wins the game.

Notes   Strategy plays a key role in this game. A player should be thinking not only of a letter which will keep him in the game, but also of one which will force the player *following him* to complete the word.

It's a good idea to keep a dictionary handy to settle any disputes about spelling.

Category "Choo Choo"

Suggested age   7 and up

Time   15 to 30 minutes

Object   To be the first player to get 5 points

Materials   Watch with second hand or two-minute egg timer

Rules   The players decide on a general category, perhaps "food and drink." The first player says any word which fits the category, such as "milk." The next player must say another food and drink which *begins* with the last letter in the word milk. One good choice is "ketchup." In the same manner, the next player supplies a food or drink which begins with the last letter in the word "ketchup." One possibility is "peach." The players take turns until one of them cannot think of a food or drink which begins with the final letter of the last player's word. (There is a two-minute time limit for responses.) When this happens, the last player who successfully thought of a word receives one point. Now the player who missed begins the second round by naming a new food or drink. Players may repeat words from a *previous* round but may not repeat them in the same round. Plurals are not permitted. An adult or older child should help younger children figure out what letter their next word starts with. The first player to get five points wins the game.

To vary the game, change the category. Be sure that your new category is broad enough for many different responses so that players don't get deadlocked too fast. Some good choices are boys' names, girls' names, animals, household objects, famous people, parts of speech, words of five letters or less, words of six letters or more, and geography terms.

My Secret Letter

Number of players 3 or more (see adaptation for 2 players below)

Suggested age 9 and up

Time 20 to 30 minutes

Object To accumulate the most points by guessing opponents' secret letters

Materials Notebook and felt pen for each player

Rules One player is chosen to be the keeper of the secret letter. He thinks of a secret letter from A to Z and writes it on the last page of his notebook. The other players write the numbers 10, 9, 8, 7, 6, 5, 4, 3, 2, 1, across a line of their notebooks. On another line, they write the letters of the alphabet from A to Z across the page.

The first player asks the keeper any question that can be answered by one word. For example, "What's your favorite ice cream flavor?" "What's your name?" "What's the first thing you're going to do when we get home?" and so on. The keeper must answer with a single word which does *not* contain his secret letter. For example, if the keeper's secret letter is Y and the questioner asks him, "How old are you?" he may say, "Ten," which, of course, doesn't contain a Y. However, if the questioner asks him, "What day is today?" he can't name a day of the week without including the letter Y. Therefore, he has to invent another answer, such as the month. (The keeper must give true answers. The only time he may give a false one is to avoid using his secret letter.)

Players take turns asking questions. On their alphabet lists they should cross off the letters in the keeper's responses, since these can't be his secret letters. For example, if the keeper answers with the word "brown," players cross the letters, B, R, O, W, and N off their lists. The player who *asked* the question also crosses off the first number (10) on his line. Players take turns asking questions, and the questioner keeps crossing off the next number on his line. A player may use his turn to guess the secret letter. If he's wrong, he crosses out his next number and the following player goes. However, if he's right, he receives the amount of points indicated by the *highest* number not yet crossed off his line. He circles that number as his score. The person who chose the secret letter also receives points—one point for *each* number that the other players have crossed out. For example, if there are two questioners and both cross out two numbers before the secret letter is guessed, the keeper receives 4 points. If the questioners cross off all their numbers without guessing the secret letter, the round is over and the keeper receives the highest possible score—in this case, 20 points (10 points for each questioner).

Players should rewrite the alphabet and the numbers from 10 to 1 for each round. When all players have had a turn to choose a secret letter, they add up their scores for all rounds. The one with the highest total score wins.

After a round if the keeper has used his secret letter by mistake in one of his answers, the other players receive 10 additional points each, and the keeper gets a zero for the round.

Strategy for the keeper The keeper should try to give the shortest responses possible or ones which contain few new letters, so that the other players can't eliminate too many letters from their alphabet lists.

He may also try to confuse the other players by giving an unexpected answer. For example, say that the keeper's secret letter is L and that a player asks him, "Are you a boy?" Instead of saying

"Yes," he may say "Sure," leading the other players to believe that his secret letter may be Y.

Strategy for questioners Players should try to select questions which force the keeper to answer with a long word or with a word which contains many different letters that have not been eliminated.

Adaptation for two players Whan two people are playing, they both think of a secret letter at the same time. Alternately, Player A questions Player B to figure out his letter, and Player B questions Player A to guess his. The first one to guess his opponent's letter wins. (Point scores are not necessary.)

Don't Say a Hundred

Suggested age 7 and up

Time 5 to 15 minutes

Object To avoid being the player to say 100

Rules The first player says any number from 1 to 10. Then the next player adds any number from 1 to 10 to the first player's number. For example, if Player A says 5 and Player B wants to add 4, he says 9. Now the next player adds a third number from 1 to 10 to the *total number* accumulated thus far. Players take turns adding numbers to the total until one player is forced to say 100. He is the loser of the game. If *more* than two people are playing, the player who loses is eliminated and the remaining players start a new round. Play continues until one player is left who hasn't said 100. He is the winner of the game.

VARIATION

Play as previously stated, except the first player to say 100 *wins* the game. For this variation, elimination rounds are not necessary.

The Traveling Clown

Suggested age 7 and up

Time 10 to 20 minutes

Object To supply descriptions of the traveling clown without breaking the clapping rhythm and to be the last player remaining in the game

Rules In this game it is important to know the order of the players. If possible, all should be sitting in the same section of the car, or in some easy-to-follow order. When players know the order of play, they all begin to clap a steady beat. The first player (in time to the beat) says, "The traveling clown is a _____ clown"—filling in the blank with a descriptive word. For example, he may say, "The traveling clown is a *funny* clown." Without breaking the rhythm or skipping a beat, the next player offers another description of the traveling clown which begins with the same letter as the first description. For example, he could say, "The traveling clown is a *fat* clown." The next player might say, "The traveling clown is a *filthy* clown." The descriptive words can be silly, but not total gibberish. For example, "The traveling clown is a *furry* clown" is acceptable, but "a flub-a-dub clown" is not, since "flub-a-dub" is not a real word. A player who can't think of an acceptable descriptive word beginning with the correct letter or who hesitates and breaks the rhythm, receives one penalty point. Then the next player (the one who goes after the player who missed) begins a new series, using a word which begins with a different letter, to describe the traveling clown.

Play with a new letter for each round. In all cases, players must use the first letter of the adjective called by the "chanter" without breaking the rhythm. Two-word descriptions are acceptable provided they fit into the rhythm of the chant—for example: "The traveling clown is a *red-haired* clown." Whenever a player has accumulated 4 penalty points, he is eliminated from the game. The last remaining player wins.

Fool Your Friends

Suggested age   7 and up

Time   20 to 35 minutes

Object   To score the most points by guessing your opponents' secret words and fooling them with your own

Materials   Felt pen and notebook for each player, watch with second hand or one-minute egg timer

Preparation   Each player selects a category from those in Chapter 3, You're on TV! (page 69). The categories should be familiar to every player in the game. Each child takes five or 10 minutes to list 10 words that fit his category. He should make sure that the other players don't see what he writes on his list (no peeking, kids!). Here are the three possible lists:

Player A musical instruments	Player B birds	Player C flowers
harp	sparrow	daisy
piano	eagle	violet
guitar	robin	rose
violin	macaw	tulip
drum	parrot	carnation
trombone	oriole	lily
oboe	woodpecker	marigold
cello	cardinal	orchid
accordion	crow	pansy
saxophone	vulture	petunia

Rules   Player A tells his category to the other players (in this case "musical instruments"). He then gives them the first and last letters of one of the words on his list. For example, he may say, "Starts with a D and ends with an M." The first player who can yell out the correct response (in this case, "drum") receives one point and records his score. If no player comes up with the right answer within one minute, the player who thought of the word receives one point. Player A goes through his entire list in this manner. There may be occasions when more than one word will fit the given letter combination. For example, "piano" and "piccolo" are both musical instruments that start with a P and end with an O. If a player calls out a legitimate but incorrect response, the one who supplied the letters simply says, "A different one," and players continue guessing. If players shout out a correct response simultaneously, both receive a point for that word. When Player A has gone through his entire list, the other players get a turn to go through their lists. Then players add up their scores. The one with the most points wins.

Adaptation for one player An adult can draw up two category skeleton lists for the single player. Each one should have 10 items and look similar to the samples shown here:

Four-legged animals

E _ _ _ _ _ _ T   G _ _ _ _ _ E
T _ _ _ R   L _ _ _ A
L _ _ N   R _ _ _ _ T
R _ _ _ _ _ R   Z _ _ _ A
A _ _ _ _ _ _ E   B _ _ R

Countries

R _ _ _ _ A   S _ _ _ N
E _ _ _ _ _ D   N _ _ _ _ _ Y
G _ _ _ _ E   C _ _ _ _ _ A
F _ _ _ _ E   I _ _ _ Y
H _ _ _ _ _ D   G _ _ _ _ _ Y

The adult should also prepare an answer sheet. The child may take five minutes to fill in the blanks on list one and another five minutes for list two. Then he checks the answer sheet and scores 5 points for each correct response. Here's a rating scale to see how well he did:

65 or under: Needs practice
70 to 80: Good
85 to 90: Very good
95 to 100: Excellent!

I Went to Visit Granny

Suggested age   8 and up (some of the variations can be enjoyed by younger children)

Time   15 to 30 minutes

Object   To be the first player to accumulate 5 points by remembering the longest series of "twin consonant" words

Materials   A pocket dictionary is helpful if you need to check spelling

Rules   The first player says the sentence, "I went to visit Granny, and I brought along a _____." The word which he chooses to fill the blank must contain two of the same consonant.   The consonants can be side by side as in the word "ta*ff*y" or separated, as in "i*c*i*c*le." For instance, the first player might say, "I went to visit Granny, and I brought along a ba*ll*." The next player must repeat the same sentence and add a double-consonant word of his own—for example, "I went to visit Granny and I brought along a ball and a *tent*." The third player repeats the sentence with the first two words and adds a third double-consonant word.   Players take turns adding words to the sentence until one player forgets the sequence or fails to think of a new response within one minute (use an egg timer or a watch with a second hand).   The last player to repeat the sequence correctly and add a word of his own gets one point.   The player who missed begins a new sequence.   Play continues until one player has won 5 points.   He is the winner of the game.

VARIATIONS

Twin-Vowel Words (ages 8 and up)

For this variation, the words which the players supply have two of the same vowel—either together (as in broom) or separated (as in engine).

Same First Letter as the Lead Word (ages 7 and up)

If the first player begins the sequence with the word "rock," all other responses for that round must begin with the letter R. The initial letter should be changed for each new round.

Same Last Letter as the Lead Word (ages 7 and up)

In this variation the words in the sequence must *end* with the same letter as the lead word.

Alphabet Sequence (ages 7 and up)

The first player's word must begin with A, the second player's with B, the third's with C, and so on. When a player misses, the next sequence begins with the letter that he missed on. When players reach the end of the alphabet, they go backward from Z to A!

Harder Variation (ages 9 and up)

The player chosen to be the starter thinks of a secret category. All items that the players name must belong to it in order to be brought to Granny's house. Categories might be things of a specific color or shape, things made of cloth or another substance, things you'd find at a birthday party, and so on. The starter mentions one item that he is bringing to Granny's house. For example, "I went to visit Granny and I brought along a light bulb." The next player must try to figure out the starter's secret category by naming an item which he would like to bring, that is, an item which has something in common with a light bulb. He might say, "I went to visit Granny, and I brought along a toaster"—another item which runs on electricity. The starter tells the player if he can come to Granny's based on whether or not the new item fits into the secret category. In this case, the starter says, "I'm sorry, but you can't come." The next player offers an item which he'd like to bring. When all players have had a turn, the starter mentions another item that he plans to bring to Granny's (perhaps, a windowpane). At this point, the next player thinks he has figured out the common thread which ties together the starter's items. Instead of suggesting another object, he uses his turn to guess the starter's secret category. He asks, "Are all of your objects made of glass?" If he is right, the round is over. The starter gets one point for each object that the other players mentioned before guessing his secret category.

Players take turns as starter—thinking of new secret categories for each round of play. When all players have had two turns to be starter, the player with the most points wins. Note that in this variation it's not necessary for players to repeat the list of items mentioned.

Stump the Stars

Number of players 3 (see the adaptation below for 4 players)

Suggested age 8 and up

Time 20 to 35 minutes

Object To get the highest "time" total by stumping the stars

Materials Felt pen and 3 × 5 index cards for each player (or you can use slips of paper instead), a watch with a second hand (or better yet, a stopwatch)

Preparation On their 10 cards players write the names of different objects or living things. The secret words should be varied and do not have to be related in any way. They must be fairly common words that the other players will know. Here's one possible list:

magician	window
sneakers	carpet
blanket	microphone
frankfurter	toothbrush
pencil	apron

Rules Unlike most of the quiz games in this book, in this one players earn scores only when they're *not* playing the game! Two players are chosen to be the "stars," and the third player is the timekeeper. The stars decide between themselves who will give clues and who will be the guesser. Once they've decided, the timekeeper gives his set of cards, face down, to the player giving the clues. At the starting signal, the clue-giver turns over the first card and gives hints to the guesser to help him find the word on the card. For example, if the first word is "magician," the clue-giver might say, "He does tricks," "He can pull a rabbit out of a hat," and so on. As soon as the guesser shouts out "magician," the clue-giver puts that card aside and goes on to the next. The clues may not contain a part of the secret word or another form of it. For example, if the clue-giver wants to elicit the word "toothbrush," he can't say, "You use this to *brush* your *teeth,*" but he can say, "You use this to clean those white things in your mouth." Nor may he *point to* an object, such as his teeth, as an added hint. If the guesser gets stuck on a word, he simply goes on to the next one. That card is put at the bottom of the pile, and he may come back to it later. When the guesser has guessed all the words he can, the two stars signal the timekeeper. He tells them how long it took them to go through the words, in minutes and seconds—for example, 2 minutes and 5 seconds. For every unguessed word, the stars receive a 30-second penalty. Thus, if two words were not guessed, the original time— in this case, 2 minutes, 5 seconds —would be changed to 3 minutes, 5 seconds. There is also a 30-second penalty for illegal clues. Let's pretend that the total time (including unguessed words and illegal clues) was 3 minutes, 5 seconds. The timekeeper records this amount as his own score. (While the stars do not earn any score for their efforts, they are trying as a *team* to get the lowest possible time, so that the timekeeper will not earn a high score.)

For the next round, the timekeeper becomes a star and one of the stars becomes the timekeeper. (In a complete game, players each get two turns to be a star and one turn to be the timekeeper.) When all the players have had a turn to be timekeeper, the one with the highest score in minutes and seconds wins the game.

Adaptation for four players When four people are playing, they break up into two teams. One team is called the timekeepers and the other the stars. (Since all four players make up word cards, each team gets two chances to be stars and two chances to be timekeepers.) The teams alternate roles as stars and timekeepers, going through one pack of their opponent's 10 word cards for each turn. After four rounds of play, the teams add their two time scores. The team with the highest score wins.

Say It With a Song!

Suggested age 4 and up

Time 5 to 20 minutes

Object To turn your ordinary conversations into songs without laughing

Rules Everyone in the car should continue his normal conversation. However, instead of *speaking* words, players must *sing* them! They can either use familiar songs or make up tunes which seem to fit their words. Any time a player laughs while singing or while listening to one of the other players sing, he gets 1 "laughing point." When a player has accumulated 3 laughing points, he can no longer win the game but should continue to play along for the fun of it. Players should sing questions to one another so that everyone is drawn into the "conversation." They can even sing the score out loud each time a player gets another laughing point.

When all players but one have 3 laughing points, the game ends. Naturally, the player with the fewest laughs wins the game.

Note This is a game that works best if everyone in the car (including the driver) plays. Somehow it spoils the mood if anyone in the car talks normally.

Players may not put hands up to their faces to conceal a laugh!

Storytelling
Word Association

Suggested age 7 and up

Time 20 to 35 minutes

Object To make up a story using all of your "association" words

Materials Notebook and felt pen for each player

Preparation Each player must write a list of 10 unrelated words in his notebook. The list should include nouns, verbs, and adjectives. The words can be types of people (such as dentist or mailman), creatures (witch, ghost), animals, objects, or places (beach, forest, cave), action words (play, sleep, crawl), or descriptive words (fat, old, round). Remember, no words like "the," "is," "and," "he," or "when," which do not suggest other words. It's fun to include a combination of words that suggest something funny or strange. Here is a sample list:

umbrella	shadow
glove	grasshopper
walk	hamburger
gun	ring
tree	book

Rules Player A reads his list of words, one at a time, to one of the other players in the car. As he reads each word, Player B must say the first thing that comes into his mind when he hears it. Player A (the one reading the list) records Player B's responses. Using the sample list, the responses might be:

umbrella—rain	shadow—stranger
glove—hand	grasshopper—insect
walk—park	hamburger—ketchup
gun—kill	ring—telephone
tree—leaves	book—read

When the association list has been completed, and a response has been recorded for each word, Player A hands the list to Player B. Player B should take a few minutes to look it over and think about how the responses he gave (*not* the original words) might be tied together into an interesting plot. Then he must tell a story to everyone in the car which uses *all* the words that he named. (He may refer to his list as he tells the tale.) The story can be funny, scary, strange, adventurous or just plain silly. Each player should have a chance to tell a story using the words that he "associated" with another player's word list. If three people are playing, Player A reads his list to Player B, Player B to Player C, and Player C to Player A. As they tell their stories, players may find it helpful to check off the words on their lists as they use them.

Adaptation for one player The single player can easily enjoy this game if an adult, even the driver, gives him associations. The single player makes a story of the associations.

Outguess the Storyteller

Suggested age 5 and up

Time 20 to 40 minutes

Object To complete an unfinished fairy tale in your own way and compare your results with the original version

Materials A short fairy tale or story which your children have never heard

Preparation Choose a short story from a book—picture books work especially well. The story should have an interesting plot and should be one your children don't know.

Rules An adult or older child in the car begins reading the story to all the players. When the reader has reached a crucial point in the story, he *stops*. (The reader should decide on this point in advance.)

Now everyone has a given number of minutes to think about how *he* would finish the story. When everyone has had enough time to think, each one should have a turn to tell his completed version of the tale. Then the reader finishes reading the actual book. As with most storytelling games, there are no winners or losers. But it's a lot of fun to discover the many roads that a single story can take! This game is especially good for children who have trouble beginning a story but do fine once the story is started.

Adaptation for one player   In advance, the adult should put a bookmark at some crucial page of a story. The single player should read the story to himself, stopping at the page which has the bookmark. Then he should put the book down and finish the story in any way he pleases. When he's done he can go back and read the published version's ending to compare the two.

Alphabet Clap-a-Story

Suggested age   6 and up

Time   15 to 30 minutes

Object   To stop your opponents from earning points by listening to their stories and *clapping* each time your hear a word that begins with the key letter

Materials   Notebook and felt pen for each player, watch with second hand or two-minute egg timer

Rules   Each player chooses a letter of the alphabet. Players take five or 10 minutes to think of a story in which many words begin with their letter. If players wish, they can jot down some of these key words in their notebooks so they will remember to include them in their stories. The stories can be nonsensical, but the sentences must fit together to make a plot.

The first player tells what his key letter is and then begins to tell a two-minute alphabet story aloud at a slow conversational pace to give the listeners time to absorb what they hear and respond to it. The other players must listen very carefully and clap each time they hear a word which begins with the key letter (there shouldn't be more than a two-word delay). Any time the storyteller's key word is not caught by the others, the storyteller tallies 2 points in his notebook, as he continues talking. And any time one or more players clap for a *wrong* word, the storyteller tallies 5 points. After two minutes, time is called and the storyteller totals his score. Then the other players take turns telling their stories. The storyteller with the highest score wins.

Strategy for creating stories Since the idea is to fool your opponents, try to include words with an initial sound similar to your key letter. For example, if you choose the letter N as your key letter, throw in a bunch of M words. Or if your letter is P, use some B words as well. Other similar sounding letters are F and V, K and Q, T and D, and E and Y. Only the sharpest of spellers will quickly be able to tell the difference between some S and C words or J and G words!

Sometimes people take short words like "a," "and," "she," "when," "the," "if," "this," and so on, for granted and fail to notice them in the context of a story. Therefore, if the first letter is right, try to include some of those little foolers.

VARIATION

Hidden Word Clap-a-Story

Each player chooses a *key word* which he will use throughout his two-minute story. Players should choose a word which might easily be confused with other words. For example, the word "mine" sounds similar to "mind," "nine," "wine," "my," and so on. Or, the word "ghost" sounds similar to "guest," "goes," "goat," "gist," "go," and so on.

In their stories, players should plan many ways to use their key words and also mix in words that sound like the key word (they may want to jot down these words before they begin so they will remember to include them). Otherwise, the game is played and scored in the same manner as the standard version.

Fairy Tale Charades

Number of players   4 or 6 (see adaptation for 2 or 3 players below)

Suggested age   7 and up (an older child or adult should help score)

Time   20 to 40 minutes

Object   To quickly act out scenes from secret fairy tales so your teammates can guess their titles

Materials   Bag with fairy tale titles, watch with second hand or, better still, a stopwatch, notebook and felt pen for scoring

Preparation   Someone not participating in the game should draw up a list of familiar fairy tales (two for each player), write their titles on separate slips of paper and place the slips in a paper bag. Here's a suggested list:

>Snow White and the Seven Dwarfs
>Goldilocks and the Three Bears
>Little Red Riding Hood
>The Wizard of Oz
>The Three Little Pigs
>Hansel and Gretel
>Cinderella
>Pinocchio
>Jack and the Beanstalk
>Rapunzel

Rules   Players should divide into two teams and decide which team will be up first. One member of Team One picks a fairy tale slip from the bag. At the starting signal, he must act out scenes from that fairy tale (either randomly or in sequence) for the other member(s) of his team. He may not just act out the title of the story. Team members try to describe the actions they are watching so the actor can let them know (without speaking) if they are on the right track. They should be cautioned not to guess titles wildly because each wrong guess will result in a 30-second penalty for the round. Of course, it isn't always easy to act things out while sitting in a car, but that's part of the fun. The actor should try to choose significant scenes from his story that will elicit a quick correct guess (for example, Cinderella trying on her glass slipper). In the meantime, Team Two is keeping time.

When the title of the story is guessed, time is called and Team One receives a time score plus a 30-second penalty for each wrong title guessed. Now a Team Two member is up, picks a new slip (don't reuse slips), and plays in the same manner as above while Team One keeps time. Note that if a team has not guessed its fairy tale after three minutes, time is called and a score recorded.

Give each team member one or two turns to be the actor and add up each team's total time when all rounds are completed. The team with the lowest time wins.

Adaptation for two or three players   With two or three players, there are no teams. The first actor follows the same procedure as above and receives a score based on how long it takes his opponents to guess his fairy tale. The opponents should try their best since the player who guesses the correct answer in a minute or less may subtract 30 seconds from his total time at the end of the game. However, the guesser who supplies a *wrong* answer must add 30 seconds to his time at the end of the game. If you aren't using a stopwatch, an adult who is not playing should keep time for each player. As in the standard version, there should be a three-minute time limit for each round. Players alternate and take one, two, or three turns each. The player with the lowest total time wins.

VARIATION

Nursery Rhyme Charades

Make slips with the titles of familiar nursery rhymes. You will need at least three slips for each player since nursery rhymes are usually easier to guess than fairy tales. Time is called after two minutes of acting instead of three minutes. Since the number of scenes in a nursery rhyme may be limited, the player can either act out the title (word by word) or act out scenes from the rhyme (or both, if necessary). The penalty for a wrong guess is ten seconds. All other rules are the same. Here's a list of nursery rhymes:

> Little Boy Blue
> Humpty Dumpty
> Georgie Porgie
> Little Miss Muffet
> Sing a Song of Sixpence
> Rock-a-Bye Baby
> Eensy-Weensy Spider
> Hey-Diddle-Diddle
> Hickory-Dickory-Dock
> Jack and Jill
> Jack-Be-Nimble
> Little Jack Horner
> Jack Sprat Could Eat No Fat
> Three Blind Mice
> The Three Little Kittens Who Lost Their Mittens

Note If your children have never played any type of charades before, try some practice motions (pouring water into a cup and drinking it, putting toothpaste onto a brush and brushing teeth, and so on) before beginning the game. Also give them a chance to act out some emotions (fear, anger, surprise). Remind them that exaggeration is the key to good mime.

Grab Bag Scenery Stories

(light traffic)

Suggested age 5 and up

Time 30 to 45 minutes

Object To create a story from the slips from 2 grab bags

Materials Notebook and felt pen for each player, 2 paper bags, small slips of paper

Preparation Write the names of five or six different types of stories on each of five or six slips of paper, and put them into bag 1. The slips might say "funny story," "sad story," "mystery," "strange story," "adventure," "fantasy." Give each player five blank slips of paper. For about 10 minutes players should look out of the window and jot down on each of their five slips one interesting object, person, building, or store that they see in the scenery. One player may write "cemetery," "mountain," "bald man," "airplane," and "old shack."

When all players have filled out their five slips, collect them and put them into bag 2.

Rules Choose for the order in which players will grab slips. Each player takes one slip from bag 1 (a story type) and five slips from bag 2. For example, one player might pick "funny story" from bag 1, and slips from bag 2 which say, "library," "motorcycle," "old lady," "McDonald's," and "traffic light." That player must now think up a comedy which uses all the five items he selected. Naturally, the other players will pick a different type of story with different items. Players have about 10 minutes to think of a story. Then one player reads his slips to the others and tells his story aloud. Each player in turn does the same. It's fascinating to see the results.

A Face Tells a Story

Suggested age 5 and up

Time 15 minutes or more

Object To observe other people on a bus, train, plane, or boat and make up stories about them

Rules Players look around and decide on one person with an interesting face or overall appearance. (They should not point to the person and should make sure that he or she is out of earshot.) Now each player takes a few minutes to create a story about the unknown person. What is his or her name? Where does he live? What kind of job does he have? What kind of family? What kind of personality? Where is that person going? On a vacation, or on some strange adventure? What will happen to him when he arrives?

When everyone has created a story about the stranger, players tell each other their tales. If they enjoyed this, they may want to pick another "character" and try again. See how funny the results of this game can be!

Materials

1. Spiral notebook for each player
2. Felt pen or crayon for each player
3. Watch with a second hand (or one- or two-minute egg timer)
4. Two paper bags
5. Storybook

Optional Materials

1. Ten 3 × 5 index cards for each player
2. Stopwatch
3. Pocket dictionary for word games

BRAINY DAY

5·BDG

GAMES

Ready to put on your thinking caps? The games in this chapter will challenge your wits with clues to uncover, puzzles to guess, and problems to solve. When your family is in the mood for a mind-boggler, you'll find something here to tickle your mental fancy.

Sweet Sixteen

Number of players 2 or more (unless instructions indicate otherwise, all games in this chapter require 2 or more players)

Suggested age 7 and up

Time 20 to 35 minutes

Object To place numbers in a 4 × 4 box in such a way that the sum of each row equals 16

Materials Notebook and felt pen for each player

Preparation Each player draws a large 4 × 4 square in his notebook to form 16 boxes

Rules The first player says any number he wishes from 1 to 12, and *all* players must write that number in any one of the 16 boxes. Now the next player says another number from 1 to 12, which all players must write in one of the remaining 15 boxes. Numbers can be repeated, but a player may never say a number which the player before him has just said. The object of the game is to place your numbers so that as many rows as possible add up to 16—horizontally, vertically, or diagonally. The players take turns saying numbers and writing them in boxes until all the boxes are filled. Then players add up the total of each of their lines (four lines horizontally, four lines vertically, and two lines diagonally) and score one point for each row which adds up to 16. A perfect score is 10. Note the sample game card.

7	3	5	4	= 19
3	6	4	3	= 16
1	2	8	5	= 16
6	5	2	4	= 17

17 = || 16 = || 19 = || 16 = ||

16 //   25 \\

Play two more rounds in the same way, drawing a new 4 × 4 square for each game, and then add up all three scores. The player with the highest total wins.

To make the game shorter or longer, you can change the number of rounds. The more players you have, the harder the game becomes.

Adaptation for one player For the single player, a parent should call out numbers from 1 to 12 at random. When the player has filled all the boxes, he figures out his score, as described above. Play three rounds in this manner and then check this chart to see how you rate:

Under 7:	Number weakling
8 to 11:	A fair number
12 to 20:	A good number
21 to 25:	An excellent number
26 to 30:	A real number whiz!

VARIATIONS

To vary your game, change the number which your lines must add up to. Call your new game, Sweet Seventeen, Sweet Nineteen, and so on. (The numbers from 16 to 21 work best.)

Category Ping-Pong

Number of players Even number (2, 4, or 6, for two teams)

Suggested age 5 and up

Time 15 to 30 minutes

Object To be the first player to score 21 points

Materials One die, paper bag with category slips, sheet of paper and felt pen to keep score, one-minute egg timer or watch with second hand

Preparation Write a category title on each of about 15 slips of paper: fruits, ice cream flavors, colors, and so on. See Chapter 3, You're on TV! (page 69), for a list of category suggestions. Make sure to choose categories which are suitable for the *youngest* child playing. On one of the slips of paper, write the words "wild card" instead of a category.

Rules Choose to determine which player (or team) will "serve" first. The server picks a category slip from the bag, calls it out, and supplies one word which fits the category. For example, if he picked "fruits," he might say "apple." Now the "ball" goes to the other player (or team), who must say a different word which fits the category—perhaps "plum." If more than two people are playing, the players on each team alternate so that everyone gets a turn. The rally continues in this manner until one player can't think of an appropriate word to fit the category (of course, repeats are not allowed). When this happens, the winning player (or team) shoots the die to determine how many points he will score for that rally. That player records his team's score on the score card, and the losing team now gets to serve. The next rally is conducted in the same way—using a new category slip (used slips are not put back in the bag). When a player picks a wild card, he may select the category players should use for that rally, though it can't be a category which has already been used. As before, when a player on one team can't think of an additional word to fit the category, the rally is over, and the winning team shoots the die to determine how many points it will receive. In the course of any rally players may not take longer than one minute to think of an appropriate response (use an egg timer or watch, if necessary). The first player or team to reach 21 points wins the game.

VARIATIONS

First-Letter Ping-Pong (ages 7 and up)

Use a bag of letter tiles, or write each letter of the alphabet on separate slips of paper or index cards. Place the slips or cards in a paper bag. The player (or team) who serves first picks a letter and must say a word which begins with that letter. Now the other player returns the serve with another word beginning with that letter, and so on. The rules of this game are the same as those of Category Ping-Pong in all other respects.

Last-Letter Ping-Pong (ages 7 and up)

This game is the same as First-Letter Ping-Pong, except that words must *end* with the letter picked (leave out the letters I, J, Q, U, and V).

Miniature Golf Judgment Games
It's About Time!

Suggested age   7 and up

Time   20 to 35 minutes

Object   To come the closest to par (or better yet, under par) for each hole on the course and end up with the *lowest* total score

Materials   Notebook and felt pen for each player, watch with a second hand or stopwatch

Preparation   Each player draws the scorecard shown here in his notebook; you don't have to draw the golf course wheel, but you will refer to it as you play the game

Rules   On this golf course, you will be judging time periods. Since most people have little idea of how long 10 seconds or 30 seconds is, it's a good idea to show players the time span of each hole before they play it. Do this by saying "start," letting the designated time elapse and then saying "stop" at the end of the time for a given hole.

Hole 1— Judging 5 seconds Par: 2	Hole 2— Judging 10 seconds Par: 3	**Golf Course**	Hole 3— Judging 15 seconds Par: 5	Hole 4— Judging 20 seconds Par: 5

Hole 5— Judging 25 seconds Par: 7	Hole 6— Judging 30 seconds Par: 8	Hole 7— Judging 35 seconds Par: 10	Hole 8— Judging 45 seconds Par: 10	Hole 9— Judging one minute Par: 15

Players take turns playing Hole 1—judging 5 seconds. A player who is *not* judging holds the watch and calls out "start." The player who is judging must yell out "stop" when he thinks 5 seconds is up. Then the timekeeper tells him how many seconds have elapsed. He receives a score based on how close he came to 5 seconds. For example, if he yelled out "stop" after 8 seconds, he would receive a score of 3, if he said "stop" after 2 seconds, he would also receive a score of 3. Naturally, the lower a player's score is, the better. You can tell how well you've done by how close you come to *par*. For example, on Hole 1, par is 2. Therefore, if a player yelled out "stop" after 7 seconds (or after 3 seconds), he would be right on par for that hole. If the player yelled "stop" after *exactly* 5 seconds, he would receive a zero, which is a perfect score. Players should enter their scores on the scorecard after each hole.

Hole	Par	My score	Hole	Par	My score
1	2		6	8	
2	3		7	10	
3	5		8	10	
4	5		9	15	
5	7		Par for the course: 65 My total _____		

When each player has had a chance to try Hole 1, check off that section of the course, and go on to play Hole 2—judging 10 seconds. Only one player can play a hole at a time, and players take turns keeping time. For Holes 6 through 9 (30 seconds to one minute), the timekeeper can *talk* to the player as he is trying to judge the passing time. This, of course, distracts the player and makes it tougher to be accurate. At any point in the conversation, the player may yell out "stop," and the timekeeper tells him how many seconds have elapsed. When all players have gone through the nine holes of the course, they add up their scores. The player with the lowest score wins the game.

Adaptation for one player The single player will need a stopwatch so he can start the timer when he's ready and stop it when he thinks the specified amount of time has elapsed. (No peeking!) He records his score by counting how many seconds his number is from the target number. Play all nine holes. How close can you come to par for the course? Can you beat your score the next time around?

How Long Am I?

Suggested age 9 and up

Time 15 to 30 minutes

Object To judge the length of different lines most accurately and obtain the *lowest* score

Materials Notebook and felt pen for each player, 12-inch ruler

Preparation Using a ruler, draw nine lines of different lengths (exact to the half inch) in one player's notebook. The length of the lines should range from one-half inch to 12 inches so they can be measured with a standard ruler. You may want to draw some vertical, some horizontal, and some diagonal lines to make things a bit more interesting. Draw perpendicular "end marks" on your lines so that there's no doubt as to where a line begins or ends.

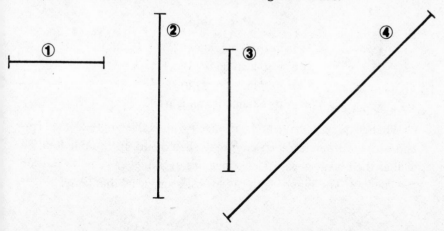

Number the lines from 1 to 9. (Don't let the players see you preparing the game or they'll know all the answers.)

Draw a scorecard in each player's notebook, leaving the par column blank for the time being.

	Par	Score		Par	Score
Line 1			Line 6		
Line 2			Line 7		
Line 3			Line 8		
Line 4			Line 9		
Line 5			Total par: My total:		

Rules Each player looks at the first line, tries to judge how long it is to the *nearest half inch,* and writes down his guess in his notebook. When everyone has done this, the line is measured. Let's say that the first line is 4 inches long. If a player guesses 2½ inches, he receives a score of 1½; if he guesses 5 inches, he receives 1 point. The player's score is based on how many inches away his guess is from the correct length. If he guesses the length exactly, he gets a perfect score of zero. Play each line in the same way, recording a score for each one. As you go along, fill in the par column, using the par table for the game.

Par Table

½-inch to 3-inch lines: Par—½
3½- to 6-inch lines: Par—1
6½- to 9-inch lines: Par—1½
9½- to 12-inch lines: Par—2

When all players have had a chance to guess the length of each line and to record par for each one, they should add up the par total as well as their own scores. How close has each player come to par for the course? The player with the lowest score wins the game.

Note that with younger children, you might prefer to make your lines exact to *the inch* instead of to the half inch. If you do this, par for a 1- to 6-inch line is *one* and for a 7- to 12-inch line, two.

Adaptation for one player The single player plays the game exactly as described above and tries to come as close as possible to par for the course or, better yet, to score under par.

People, Places, and Things

Suggested age 6 and up

Time 15 to 45 minutes, depending on the number of rounds

Object To figure out your opponent's secret word with a minimum of wrong guesses and collect the most money

Materials Notebook and felt pen for each player

Preparation On a sheet of notebook paper, each player should write the following amounts of money in this order: $100, $95, $90, $85, $80, $75, $70, $65, $60, $55, $50, $45, $40, $35, $30, $25, $20, $15, $10, $5, and $0.

If you use play money, bring along 10 $50 bills, 15 $20 bills, and 20 $10 bills.

Rules One player is chosen to be it. He must think of a secret word which is either a person, place, or thing. If he chooses a person, it can be either a famous personality or someone whom all the players know (a neighbor, friend, or relative). If he chooses a place, it can be either a specific city, state, country, mountain, river, and so on or a general kind of place such as a beach, amusement park or zoo. If he chooses a thing, it can be either an inanimate object (ball, keys, television set) or a living thing (a specific plant or animal).

When the player has thought of his secret word, he must tell the other players whether it is a person, place, or thing. He should make sure that it is a word that even the youngest player knows. One of the other players now asks him a question about his word. It must be a question which can be answered by yes or no. Let's say the secret word is "Aunt Bessie." The first questioner may ask, "Is it a famous person?" If the answer is no, *everyone* crosses out $100, so that the highest amount of money left is $95. Now it's the next questioner's turn (or if only two people are playing, the same questioner continues). Perhaps the next question is, "Is it a relative of ours?" Since the answer to that question is yes, the $95 is not crossed out and that *same* questioner can ask another question. As long as he gets yes answers, he can keep asking questions without crossing out any money values. However, as soon as one of his questions is answered with a no, the next money value is crossed out by all, and the next questioner takes his turn.

At any time during a questioner's turn (except when he's just received a no answer), he may try to guess the secret word. If he's wrong, everyone crosses off the highest dollar value, and the next player goes. However, if he's right, he receives the highest money value shown as his score (you can use play money if you want, or simply write down a money score). The player who thought of the word also receives a money score—$5 for every amount that was crossed out before the questioner guessed his word. For example, if the winning questioner received a $60 score, the player who thought of the word would receive $40 (the two amounts always add up to $100).

Now another player is it and thinks of a different secret word. When everyone has had a chance to be it, players add up their money scores (or count their play money). The player with the most money wins the game.

For a longer game, you may prefer giving each player two or three turns to be it.

VARIATIONS

Guess My Job

Played like People, Places, and Things except that the secret word must be a specific occupation (dogcatcher, baker, minister, and so on).

Surprise Bag Guessing Game

The person who is "it" puts a small object found in the car, inside a paper bag while everyone else hides his eyes. The other players must try to guess the object in the bag. The rules are the same as the standard version, except that if no one has guessed the hidden object by the time $50 has been crossed out, questioners may shake the bag as an added hint.

Monkey See, Monkey Do

Suggested age   4 and up

Time   10 to 20 minutes

Object   To be the first player to score 5 points by correctly remembering and touching the longest sequence of objects

Materials   Felt pen and paper to keep score (optional)

Rules   Before beginning this game, an adult should limit the playing area so there won't be too much jumping around the car. The first player starts the game by touching any object in the car he wishes—for example, one of the windows. The next player has to touch that same object (in this case, the same window) plus a new one, perhaps a road map. The next player must touch the two things that have already been touched plus a third, perhaps his own right ear. Play continues until one player touches the objects out of sequence or can't remember what they are. The last player to successfully touch all the objects in sequence receives one point. Now the player who was out begins a new sequence, which is played in the same way. The game continues until one player has earned 5 points. He is the winner of the game. If more than two people are playing, the remaining players can try for second and third place.

If a much younger child is playing, he can be spotted a point or two to make the game fairer.

VARIATIONS

Funny Motions, Funny Faces

For this variation, the players must repeat a series of motions or exaggerated facial expressions (either funny or serious) instead of touching objects. The first player may scratch his left underarm with his left hand. The next player must repeat that motion and then add one of his own. The third player must repeat the first two and add a third and so on. In all other ways, this version is the same as Monkey See, Monkey Do.

Baby Talk

For this variation, the players must be able to repeat a series of nonsense words or unusual sounds (players should *not* use real words). The first player may say "blip." The second player must repeat that sound and add one of his own. The next player repeats the first two and adds a third, and so on. Otherwise, this version is also the same as Monkey See, Monkey Do.

Eye Witness

Suggested age   7 and up (children from 4 to 6 can play the easier version of this game)

Time   20 to 35 minutes

Object   To remember and identify the details in a picture

Materials   Notebook and felt pen for each player, four photographs or pictures cut out of magazines or newspapers

Preparation   Cut four different pictures out of a magazine or newspaper or find four interesting family photos. The best type of picture is one with a variety of action or detail. Color pictures are better than black and white ones. Put your pictures into a large envelope or paper bag.

Rules Each player numbers his paper from 1 to 20. Take out one of the pictures and give the children a minute or two to study it. Then put the picture away and ask the players five different questions about what they saw in the picture. After each question the players write their answers in their notebooks. The type of questions you ask will depend on the picture you use. Some possibilities are: What color was a specific thing in the picture? How many of a certain thing were there in the picture (buttons on a boy's coat, people smiling, people wearing hats)? What was the location of a specific item or person (on the floor, leaning against the wall, on the window sill)? What was a specific person (or animal) doing or wearing? You can also ask about details in the picture, such as: What time did the clock say? Was the door open or closed? Was there a carpet on the floor? If you wish, some of your questions can require true or false answers.

The difficulty of your questions depends on the ages of the players. If their ages vary greatly, ask the younger child an easier set of questions than the older one, using the same pictures for both. You will probably have to record the younger child's answers for him. The questioner may look at the picture when he asks the questions, but he should write them down so he won't forget what they are.

When you've asked all five questions and the players have recorded their answers, show them the second, third, and fourth picture. Ask five questions about each one. Then the players may look at the pictures again and score their answer sheets. They receive 5 points for each correct answer—100 points is a perfect score. The player with the highest score wins the game.

If a parent would rather not participate in the game as questioner, he can write down the five questions for each picture in advance or the children can quiz each other. If two children are playing, use eight pictures instead of four. Each player can question the other on four different pictures. With three players or more, players should divide into two teams. With three players, have the oldest child compete against the younger two. The team with two members should average their score and compare it to their opponent's score.

Adaptation for one player A child can play this game alone if an adult questions him or writes down the questions on separate index cards in advance. When the player has answered the questions for all four pictures, he can take them out again to mark his answer sheet (5 points for each correct answer). He might enjoy looking at the following rating scale:

Under 50: You're not a detective
50 to 60: Fair
65 to 75: Pretty good, Sherlock
80 to 90: Congratulations, sharp eyes!
95 or 100: A perfect "Eye Q!"

Climb the Skyscraper

Suggested age 7 and up

Time 30 to 40 minutes

Object To be the first player to reach the top of the skyscraper

Materials Letter slips or commercial letter tiles, notebook and felt pen for each player, two-minute egg timer or watch with second hand

Preparation One player draws the skyscraper shown here into his notebook. There should be 25 stories in the building, divided into as many sections as you have players. (The skyscraper here is for a three-person game.)

If you don't own commercial letter tiles, make up 34 letter slips for each letter of the alphabet and an extra one for each vowel (A, E, I, O, U, and Y). Leave two of the slips completely blank. Write the following point values on the corners of each letter slip:

A: 1 point	H: 3 points	O: 1 point	V: 4 points
B: 2 points	I: 1 point	P: 3 points	W: 3 points
C: 3 points	J: 5 points	Q: 7 points	X: 7 points
D: 2 points	K: 5 points	R: 2 points	Y: 4 points
E: 1 point	L: 2 points	S: 2 points	Z: 7 points
F: 3 points	M: 4 points	T: 2 points	
G: 2 points	N: 3 points	U: 3 points	

Put all the slips into a paper bag.

Rules Pick seven letter tiles or slips from the bag, and give each player a chance to write the letters and their point values in his notebook (if you are using commercial letter tiles, use the point values on the tiles). For a sample game, let's use this draw: L (2), T (2), V (4), O (1), E (1), I (1), M (4).

Sample Skyscraper Game

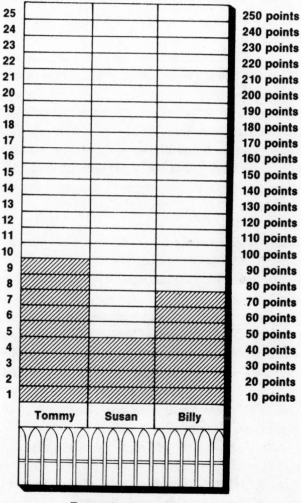

Tommy's score: 86
Susan's score: 43
Billy's score: 65

At the starting signal, players have two minutes to write down as many words as they can of three letters or more which contain any or all of the seven letters. At the end of two minutes, play stops, and players figure their scores by adding up the point values of the letters in the words they have made. For example, using the letters in the sample draw, a player might make the following words and score: "vote" (8 points), "move" (10 points), "mile" (8 points), "time" (8 points), "lit" (5 points), "love" (8 points), "tile" (6 points), "vomit" (12 points), "live" (8 points), "toe" (4 points), "melt" (9 points). The total score is 86. As in other letter games in this book, words can be written in only one form on any one list—for example, "meet" or "met," but not both. Proper nouns, slang words, and abbreviations are not permitted.

When players have figured out their scores for that hand and have checked each other's words and scores, they start filling in the skyscraper. Players round off their scores to the nearest 10 and fill in one floor on their section of the skyscraper for every 10 points they earned. For example, the player whose sample hand is shown received a score of 86. Rounded off to the nearest 10, his score is 90. Therefore, he may fill in the *first nine floors* in his section of the skyscraper. (Scores from 80 to 84 would be rounded off to 80. Scores of 85 to 90 would be rounded off to 90.)

Now players begin a second round by picking seven letters again. If a hand contains a blank slip, players can use it to stand for any letter they wish. However, once a player has decided what letter he wants his blank slip to stand for, he can use it only for that letter in that round. Blank slips are worth 3 points, no matter what letter they stand for. When all players have chosen the letter that their blank slip will stand for, the contest begins as usual. (Naturally, players may choose different letters for their blank slips since they don't consult with one another about their letters or blanks.)

Each time a round is completed and scores are totaled, players fill in more floors of their skyscraper section. Play continues until one player has reached the 25th floor. He is the winner of the game.

Notes If a hand of seven letters has either no consonants or no vowels and no blank slips, put the seven letters back into the bag, and pick a new set of letters.

If children of seven or eight are playing with older children or adults, allow them to include two-letter words. You may also want to spot them five floors or more to make the game more challenging for the older players. (The child should color his "free" floors before the game begins.)

Adaptation for one player The object of the game for the single player is to reach the top of the building with as few letter hands as possible. He can check this chart to see how well he did:

9 or 10 hands: Better stick to anthills!
7 or 8 hands: With exercise you'll improve
5 or 6 hands: A good steady climber
3 or 4 hands: The human fly should step aside!
1 or 2 hands: Today a skyscraper, tomorrow the world!

Let's See You Do Better!

Suggested age 7 and up

Time 30 to 45 minutes

Object To score the most points by making words with your own and other players' letters

Materials Notebook and felt pen for each player, bag of commercial letter tiles (or letter slips) and two-minute egg timer or watch with second hand

Preparation None, if you have commercial letter tiles. Otherwise, make up 34 letter slips as described in the previous game, Climb the Skyscraper.

Rules This is the perfect game for kids or adults who are always complaining that they lose word games because of "bad letters." Choose to see who will go first. The first player picks seven letters from the bag, writes them down in his notebook, and then returns the letters to the bag. He should write his seven letters and their point values inside seven boxes. For a sample game let's use these letters and values: O (1), D (2), N (3), R (2), I (1), A (1), and E (1).

The player now has two minutes to form any one word of two letters or more, using the letters on his page. Proper nouns, slang words, and abbreviations are not permitted. When time is called, the player shows his word to the other players and records a score for it by adding up the point values of the letters. If he uses up all his letters, he receives a bonus of 25 points. Now all of the other players try to form a different word with the letters in Player One's hand. He calls out his seven letters, along with point values, and the other players write them down in their notebooks. They have two minutes to write a *different* word with the letters in Player One's hand. Let's say that Player One made the word "ride." Other possible words in this hand are "drain," "rained," "earn," "radio," and "read." The words which the other players make cannot simply be a different form of Player One's word, such as "rode." When time is called, the other players read (and spell) the words they formed. If their words are all different (and legitimate), they also record a score for Player One's hand. However, if more than one of the players formed the same new word, they receive no score for it (no peeking during play). If Player One's hand contains a blank slip, it may be used to stand for any letter and is worth 5 points. When opposing players take their turn at his hand, they can also make the blank stand for any letter. Just as Player One receives a bonus of 25 points for seven-letter words, so do his opponents if they are able to use all of Player One's letters to make a different word.

If at the end of two minutes, Player One can't think of any word with the letters in his hand, the other players still get a chance to try to do so. If the other players *can* think of words (and they are all different), they record scores for Player One's hand. However, if none of the players can form a word with that hand, Player One may pick seven new letters and begin again.

After all players have had a chance at Player One's hand, Player Two takes seven new letters from the bag and leads off a new round. Of course, the player who leads the hand has two advantages over the others—he gets first crack at the letters, and he doesn't have to worry about duplicating a word.

Play continues in this manner until each player has had five chances to be up. At the end of five rounds, the player with the highest score wins. For a shorter game, play three or four rounds.

I'm No Square!

Suggested age 7 and up

Time 20 minutes

Object To be the player to find the most squares in the puzzle picture

Materials One copy of the square diagram and a few crayons or magic markers for each player (if these are unavailable, a single felt pen for each player)

Preparation Players draw the diagram shown into their notebooks. It should have eight boxes across and eight boxes down—a total of 64 boxes.

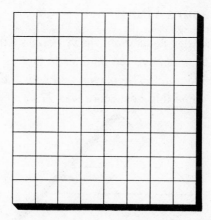

Rules At the starting signal, players have 15 minutes to find as many squares as they can in their diagrams. They can be squares of any size. (A square must contain the same number of boxes down as

it does across. The small original boxes also count as squares.) Players should outline the squares with different colored magic markers, using a different color for each size, if possible. They should also make a tally of the squares they've counted. At the end of the time limit, the player who has found the most squares wins the game. Players must be able to prove how many they've found by pointing them out to the others! At last count, I found 204.

Adaptation for one player   As in the standard version, the single player studies the square diagram and tries to find as many squares as possible. He may want to check this rating scale to see how well he did:

> Under 85: Weak
> 85 to 100: Fair
> 101 to 125: Good
> 126 to 150: Very good
> 151 to 175: You're no square!
> 176 to 200: Excellent
> Over 200: Expert!

VARIATION

Triangle Treasure Hunt

Players draw the triangle diagram shown here into their notebooks. For this variation players have ten minutes to find as many triangles as they can in the diagram. The player who finds the most (and can prove it) wins the game (My best score was 77.)

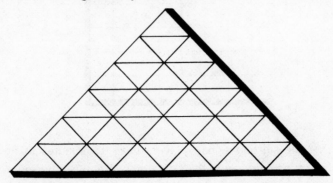

Adaptation for one player The single player follows the procedure of the standard version. He can check this rating scale to see how well he did.

Under 45: Weak
45 to 55: Fair
56 to 60: Good
61 to 65: Very good
66 to 70: Excellent
Over 70: Expert!

Dice Combinations

Suggested age 6 and up

Time 10 to 30 minutes

Object To be the first player to shoot two number combinations for each number from 2 to 12

Materials A pair of dice in a clear glass jar, notebook and felt pen for each player

Preparation Each player writes the numbers from 2 to 12 in a single column in his notebook

Rules Choose to see who will go first. The first player shakes the dice, adds the numbers, and draws a check next to the total on his notebook page. For example, if the player shoots a 3 and 4, he draws a check next to the number 7. The other players take their turns in the same way. If a player rolls a number that he's already checked two times, he forfeits his turn.

To win the game, players need to check each number from 2 to 12 twice. The first player to do so wins the game.

Occasionally, this game drags out longer than you'd like. If so, set a time limit (20 to 30 minutes), and if *no* player has finished at the end of that period, the player with the most checks wins the game.

Egg Carton Games

The two games which follow are played with an egg carton shaker. To make one, all you have to do is to take an ordinary cardboard egg carton with a solid top (no holes), write the necessary numbers or letters in the bottom of the 12 cups, and drop in the number of beans or marbles that the game requires. To use your shaker, simply close the top, shake the carton, and open it up to see what you get. The egg carton shaker adds a novel twist when your gang is tired of dice and spinners.

Egg Carton Make-a-Word

Suggested age   7 and up

Time   15 to 45 minutes

Object   To get the highest score by making the most and longest words with the letters in the egg carton

Materials   Egg carton shaker with 7 marbles or beans, notebook and felt pen for each player

Preparation   Write one letter in each cup of your egg carton. You can use the letters suggested here or others, as long as you include at least three vowels.

Rules   One of the players shakes the egg carton and opens it to see where the seven marbles or beans have landed. Naturally, two or more marbles may land in the same letter cup. If *none* of the marbles

land in a vowel, shake again. Otherwise, all players write down the seven letters and have five minutes to make as many words as possible of three letters or more from those letters. Players score one point for each letter in all the words they make.

Let's say the letters N, E, E, T, L, A, and P came up. One list might look like this, for a score of 55 points:

tale	eat
pale	neat
peel	net
plant	plate
planet	ton
pant	pet
tea	late

Play five rounds in the same manner. All players work with the same combination of letters for each round. Always shake again if *no* vowels or no consonants appear. The player with the highest total score after five rounds of play wins the game.

Younger children should be permitted to make two-letter words. You can also spot them a few points when they're playing with older players.

Adaptation for one player Play two sets of three rounds. Try to improve your score the second time around.

Egg Carton Twenty-One

Suggested age 7 and up

Time 15 to 30 minutes

Object To come as close as possible to 21 without going *over*

Materials Notebook and felt pen for each player, egg carton with one marble or bean

Preparation   Number the cups in an egg carton from 1 to 12 in the order shown here, and put one marble or bean inside.

1	8	3	10	5	12
7	2	9	4	11	6

Rules   The first player shakes the egg carton, opens it, and records the number he has shot. He shouldn't show his first number to the other players, although he must show them subsequent numbers. If the first number is 9 or less, he will certainly want to shake again, since he wants to come as close as possible to a total of 21 without going over. For example, let's say the player shakes an 8, decides to go again, and shakes a 5 the second time. He now has a total of 13, though the other players don't know his total since they don't know his first number. If he wants to take a risk, he can try for a higher number closer to 21, or he can stick with 13. If he shoots again, he must get an 8 or less to stay on or under 21. Whether he sticks to his score or rolls again, he doesn't reveal his total to the others.

The remaining players take their turns in the same way, recording their scores as they play. When all have had a turn with the shaker, the players reveal their hands. The one who comes the closest to 21 without going over wins the game. In case of a tie, players take turns shaking the carton and high number wins.

After seven rounds, the player who wins the most games is the champ.

Adaptation for one player   Play seven "hands." Any score of 21 or less is recorded at face value (for example, a score of 13 receives 13 points). However, any score *over* 21 receives a zero. After seven rounds of play, total your score. How do you rate?

Under 100:   Poor
100 to 110:   Fair
111 to 120:   Good
121 to 130:   Very good
131 to 140:   Excellent
141 to 147:   Expert!

Spin-a-Score Word Contest

Suggested age   7 and up (an older player should help score)

Time   30 to 45 minutes

Object   To make the most words with the letters you pick and score the most points

Materials   Notebook and felt pen for each player, bag of commercial letter tiles or letter slips, standard spinner numbered 1 to 6 or die in a clear glass jar, watch to keep time

Preparation   None, if you have commercial letter tiles. Otherwise, make 32 letter slips—one for each of the letters from A to Z and an extra one for each of the vowels, including Y. To make the slips, tear three pages out of a spiral notebook and rip them into 32 pieces. Put all of your letter slips into a paper bag.

Rules   Each player in turn, picks 10 letter tiles or slips from the bag, writes the letters into his notebook and then returns them to the bag. If any player picks a hand without vowels or without consonants, he may return his letters to the bag and pick again. When all players have recorded 10 letters, they have 10 minutes (or 15 minutes if you prefer) to write down as many words as they can of three letters or more, using *only* the letters that appear in their hands. Children eight or under should be allowed to make two-letter words as well. Naturally, everyone's hand is different.

   At the end of the time limit, there is a "spin off" to determine the point value of each letter. The letters that appear in one or several of the players' hands are called out one at a time, and a player spins the spinner for each one. Let's say an E was called out and the number 4 was spun. The letter E will be worth 4 points for all of the players who have it. Do this for *every* letter that appears in one or more of the players' hands.

   Now players write a score for each of their words, based on the point values of the letters. They add up all their word scores, and the player with the highest total wins the game.

Adaptation for one player Try this game twice—picking different letters and spinning different point values each time. Can you beat your own score?

VARIATION

For a more competitive game, have all the players work with the *same* 10 letters. When a player picks the letters that will be used, everyone writes them down.

Escape From Big Foot

Suggested age 7 and up

Time 10 to 30 minutes

Object To arrive home safely without being caught by Big Foot

Materials One game path, felt pen for each player, spinner or die

Preparation Draw the game path below into one player's notebook. Make a lane for each player. There should be 15 boxes across,

Big Foot Path for Three Players

including the first column with the foot and the last column with the house. In the fourth column on the path, each player should write his name. Each player should place a dot somewhere on his row (the dots should not be in line with each other).

Rules An adult or older child gives the first player a word to spell. The list of spelling words doesn't have to be made up in advance—just choose an object in the scenery. Make sure the words are within the child's capabilities. (If your children can't spell yet, ask them the first or last letter of a word.)

If the player spells his word correctly, he may put an X in the first box after his name box. If he's wrong, he remains in the name box. Then the rest of the players get turns to spell their first words. When each player has been given one question, Big Foot moves ahead one space. To move him, draw another foot in the entire second column.

Now each player gets a second word to spell. As before, any player who spells his word correctly may move into the next box along his path by drawing an X in it (otherwise, he stays put). When every player has had a second turn, Big Foot is moved forward another box by drawing a foot in the entire third column.

Big Foot moves forward one column after every round of questioning. (In the fourth column just draw the foot right over the players' names.) When a player arrives at his dotted box, he calls out a number from 1 to 6. If he spins that number on the spinner (or on the die) he gets an extra turn. He is given another word to spell, and if correct, he may move ahead another box. However, if any other number comes up, he loses his turn in the next round, and Big Foot moves one step closer to him.

Whenever Big Foot catches up to a player, that player is eliminated from the game. The remaining player or players continue as before. Any player who arrives safely inside his house wins the game. This is one game that can have more than one winner (or no winners).

Adaptation for one player The single player follows the same rules as above. Naturally, an adult or older child must supply his spelling words.

Escape From the Burning Building

Suggested age 4 and up (an older child or adult should keep time)

Time 20 to 40 minutes

Object To escape the fastest from the burning building

Materials One game picture, felt pen and paper to record times, watch with a second hand (or, better yet, a stopwatch)

Preparation Draw the game path below with a window and ladder for each player. Each ladder should have eight rungs. For a longer or shorter game, make more (or fewer) rungs.

Rules   As we all know, if you're trying to escape from a burning building, the faster you get out, the better! To set the escape in motion, an adult or older child gives an arithmetic problem out loud to the player at the first window on the left of the building. As soon as the player gets his problem, the questioner times how many seconds it takes him to respond with the correct answer. The problem can be addition, subtraction, multiplication, or division, depending on what the child can handle. With younger children, you can ask the number that comes next in a series or any question involving counting.

If a player calls out the wrong answer, someone who knows the answer (or the questioner) yells out, "No good," and the player keeps guessing. Let's say it took the first player 20 seconds to give a correct answer in round one. He would write "20 seconds" on the top rung of his ladder. The longest a player may take for any one response is two minutes. If the player can't come up with the correct answer within that time he writes "two minutes" on that rung of his ladder.

Everyone gets one question and records a time for it before round two questions begin. Play continues for eight rounds. When all players have recorded a time on each rung of the ladder, they add up their total time in minutes and seconds. The player who escapes the fastest from the burning building (the lowest score) wins the game.

Adaptation for one player   The single player must have someone to question him. If the driver is the questioner, the player can keep time for himself. After recording a score on each rung, he can look on this chart to see how well he did:

Over 13 minutes: Burned to a crisp!
11 to 13 minutes: Full of blisters
8 to 11 minutes: Barely beat the heat
6 to 8 minutes: A bit hot but fine
4 to 6 minutes: A clean break
2 to 4 minutes: A cool escape artist
Under 2 minutes: You're a mental Houdini!

Life Is a Puzzle

Suggested Age 7 and up

Time 15 to 30 minutes

Object To get your "life" together in the shortest amount of time

Materials Four "life" letters for each player (each in a separate envelope), a notebook for each child to lean on, and a watch to keep time

Preparation Directions for one set of "life" letters: Trace the letters shown below onto the unlined side of four separate 3 × 5 index cards. It doesn't matter if the kids watch you prepare the puzzle—"life" will still be a challenge. After you've traced the four letters, cut them out carefully along all the solid lines and put the pieces for each letter into a separate envelope. Label each envelope by letter so you'll know which contains which pieces.

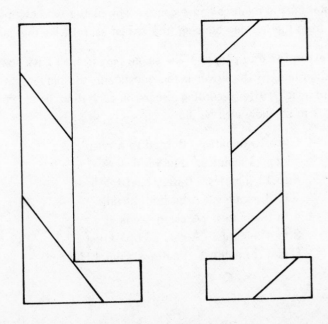

Rules   Give each player an L envelope.   At the starting signal, players must remove the four pieces from their envelopes and try to put the letter L together.   As soon as a player is finished, he shows it to an adult in the car (to check if it's correct), and receives his next envelope, the letter I.   When he's finished the I correctly, he goes on to the F and then to the E.   The player who can put his "life" together first wins the game.   The other players may continue playing for second place, third place, and so on.   Don't feel like a failure if you quit in frustration—no one ever said that "life" was easy!

Materials

1. Spiral notebook for each player
2. Felt pen or crayon for each player
3. Watch with a second hand (for most games, you can use a one- or two-minute egg timer instead)
4. Two paper bags
5. Dice in a clear glass jar (for most games, you can use a spinner or playing cards)
6. Egg carton and seven marbles or beans

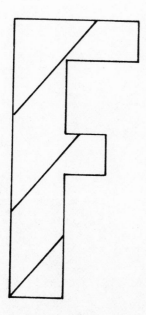
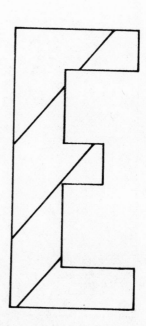

7. Four photographs or pictures from newspapers or magazines
8. 12-inch ruler
9. Four index cards for each player
10. Four envelopes for each player
11. Scissors

Optional Materials

1. Commercial letter tiles
2. Play money
3. Stopwatch
4. Different colored crayons or magic markers

A PACK OF
6·PCG
CARD GAMES

Tired of Old Maid and Go Fish? The card games in this chapter bear little resemblance to the kind you've played before. Some are solitaire games that can be enjoyed by one or more players, and others are games for two or more with unusual twists to delight children of all ages. They have all been specially adapted for play in a moving vehicle. With no further ado, let's take a look at what's in the cards.

Grab Bag Poker

Number of players 2 or more

Suggested age 8 and up

Time 15 to 25 minutes

Object To complete the most poker combinations

tal, 5 vertical and 2 diagonal "poker hand" rows and score the most points

Materials Notebook and felt pen for each player, standard deck of playing cards, two paper bags

Preparation One of the players draws a 5 × 5 square into his notebook. Shuffle your deck of cards and place it in one of the paper bags; save the other bag for discards.

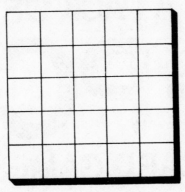

Note There are some differences between this game and regular poker that you should be aware of as you read the rules. In regular poker, you play with a hand of cards, but in Grab Bag Poker, you pick one card at a time and record the number and suit in one of the 25 boxes of the 5 × 5 square. To make things easy, write J for jack, Q for queen, K for king and A for ace. In regular poker a player gets five (or seven) cards and tries to form the best possible combination with the whole hand, but in Grab Bag Poker, a player can record a score for the first two or three cards in a line, if they make a scoring combination.

Rules The first player picks a card from the bag, writes the number and suit in any one of the 25 boxes, and puts the card in the discard bag. The next player picks another card from the grab bag, writes the number and suit in one of the 24 remaining boxes and discards it. Players continue taking turns in this manner. Any time the card that a player fills in *completes* a scoring poker combination in one of the ows (horizontally, vertically, or diagonally), he records a score for the combination in his notebook. (Refer to the table for the scoring combinations and their point values.)

Point Values

Pair (2 of a kind):	10 points
2 Pairs:	25 points
3 of a kind:	30 points
Flush (5 of the same suit):	35 points
4 of a kind:	45 points
Straight (5 consecutive numbers):	50 points
Full house (3 of a kind and 2 of a kind):	50 points
Straight Flush (5 consecutive numbers of the same suit):	75 points
Royal Flush (10, jack, queen, king, and ace of the same suit):	100 points

Let's say the board looks like the one shown here, and the player has just picked a queen of hearts. If he writes queen of hearts in any one of the starred boxes, he records 10 points for a pair of queens. Note that the two queens do not have to be in adjacent boxes, as long as they're in the same straight line.

When players write down a card, they should try to place it in a position which will lead to a scoring poker hand. For example, in the diagram the 5, 6, and 8 are in one straight line. If a player picks a 4, 7, or 9, he should write it in the same line to try for a straight points). Of course, the only person who receives credit fr straight is the player who *completes* it by writing in the last necessary number. In the second horizontal row, players are trying for a flush by filling in all diamonds. Naturally, some of these plans won't work out.

It *is* possible for the same player or two different players to score more than one poker combination in the *same* row. For example, say that one player has recorded 10 points for a pair of queens in one straight line and later another player picks a third queen. If there's still an opening for him to write down the third queen in the same line, he may record 30 points for three of a kind. It's even possible to score three different combinations in the same row (a pair, two pairs, and then a full house).

If a player completes a scoring combination in *more than one row,* he receives credit for both of the combinations that he has completed. For example, if the board looks like the one here and the player picks a 5 of hearts, he can make two combinations by placing it in the starred box (a flush and a pair).

3♡				
	✱			
	5◇	6♡		
			10♡	
				Q♡

When all 25 boxes have been filled, the players add up their scores. The player with the highest total wins.

Solitaire Version The single player draws a 5 × 5 square and puts his shuffled cards into one of the paper bags. As in the standard version, he fills in the 25 boxes with the cards he picks, trying to make poker combinations in the 12 rows. However, *unlike* the standard version, he does *not* record scores as he goes along, but instead, at the *end* of the game. He can score only *one* poker combination per row. If any one row has more than one possibility, he chooses the combination that yields the highest score.

Sample Game of
Grab Bag Solitaire Poker

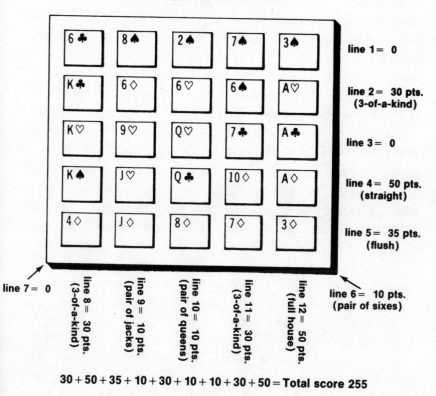

$30 + 50 + 35 + 10 + 30 + 10 + 10 + 30 + 50 =$ **Total score 255**

Under 30—Over 40

Number of players 2 (any number can play the solitaire version which follows)

Suggested age 9 and up

Time 15 to 25 minutes

Object To lay out the cards so they will total as much *under* 30 points or as much *over* 40 points as possible in your 6 assigned rows and to prevent your opponent from doing so in his 6 rows

Materials Notebook and felt pen for each player, standard deck of playing cards, and two paper bags

Preparation Draw a 5 × 5 square into one of the player's notebooks as in the previous game. Shuffle your deck of playing cards, and place it in one of the paper bags (save the other bag for discards).

Note As in Grab Bag Poker, the cards that players pick are recorded one at a time, on the 5 × 5 square. For this game, only the *numbers* of the cards are recorded, not the suits. To save room, write J for jack, Q for queen, K for king, and A for ace. Aces count as one point, number cards at face value, and pictures as 10 points.

Rules Have you ever gone to an amusement park or carnival and played the game in which you roll balls (or throw darts) at numbers to total less than 11 or more than 30? Pretty tough to win, isn't it? Well, this game is based on the same idea, although you have complete control over where the cards go.

One of the players is assigned all the vertical rows and one diagonal row of a 5 × 5 square, and the other player is assigned all the horizontal rows and the other diagonal row.

The first player picks a card from the paper bag, writes the number in any one of the 25 boxes, and then puts the card in the "discard" bag. The second player goes in the same manner. The players take turns picking cards and recording them, keeping in mind that their objective is to total as much *over* 40 points or as much *under* 30 points as they can in their six assigned rows. If possible, a player should avoid making his own rows total 30, 40, or anything in between, since these will earn *minus* points, but he should try to spoil his opponent's rows by doing so.

When all of the boxes have been filled in, players figure out their scores in the following way. Player One adds and records six scores—the total of each vertical row and his assigned diagonal row. Player Two also adds and records six scores—the total of each horizontal row and his assigned diagonal row.

If the total point value of a row is *under 30*, the score for that row is based on *how much under 30* the total is. For example, if one of the rows adds up to 22 points, the player's score for that row is 8 (30 − 22 = 8). If the total point value of a row is *over 40*, the score for that row is based on *how much over 40* the total is. For example, if one of the rows adds up to 45 points, the player's score for that row is 5 (45 − 40 = 5).

If a row totals *exactly* 30 or 40, the player receives −10 for that row. If the total of any row is *between 30 and 40*, the player's *minus* score is the *number of points over 30* which the row totals. For example, if a row adds up to 34 points, the player gets −4.

Once the players have determined their scores for their six rows, they subtract the total of their minus scores from the total of their plus scores to get their final totals. This may be a plus or a minus number. The player with the best plus score wins. (If no one gets a plus score, the *lowest* minus score wins.) Our family found this to be a rather low scoring game. If you can get more than 15, you've done well. More than 20 is terrific! See the diagram below for a sample game.

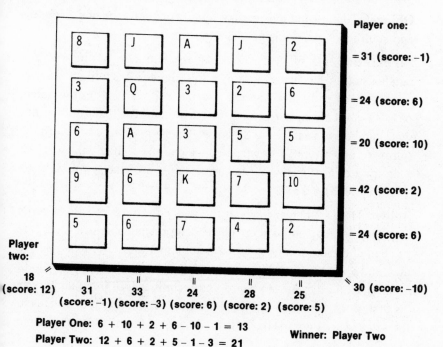

Player One: 6 + 10 + 2 + 6 − 10 − 1 = 13
Player Two: 12 + 6 + 2 + 5 − 1 − 3 = 21

Winner: Player Two

Solitaire Version The single player plays the same game as above, except that he picks all 25 cards himself and works with 12 rows instead of six. In each of five horizontal, five vertical, and two diagonal rows, he will be trying to score *over 40* or *under 30*, avoiding scores of 30, 40, or anything in between.

The highest possible score is 158, and the lowest is –120, but it isn't likely that you'll approach either extreme. If you score over 35 in the solitaire version, you should be very proud of yourself (over 45 is a highly respectable score for adults).

It All Adds Up to Fun!

Number of players 2 or more

Suggested age 9 and up

Time 10 to 15 minutes

Object To earn the most points by crossing out high-point addition and subtraction problems on a 5 × 5 square

Preparation Draw a 5 × 5 square into one of the player's notebooks (see the first diagram in this chapter). Shuffle a deck of playing cards and place them in a paper bag. To set up the game, pick 25 consecutive cards from the bag (one at a time) and record their numbers in each of the 25 boxes (it's not necessary to record the suit or to pay attention to which boxes you place them in).

In the explanations which follow, aces (A) are ones, two's to ten's are face value, jacks (J) are 11, queens (Q) are 12, kings (K) are 13.

Rules The first player looks at the playing square for sets of cards which will form an addition or subtraction problem and its answer (the position of the cards on the board is not important). For example, he may find a 6 and a 5, adding up to 11 (jack). He then crosses the 6, 5, and jack off the playing board and records those three numbers as his first score, for a total of 22 points. Now the next player goes in the same way. Perhaps he finds a 13 (king), a 9, and a 4; subtracting the 4 from the 13, he gets a 9. He then crosses off the king, 4, and 9 from the board and records the three numbers for a score of 26 points. A player is also allowed to say, "7 − 7 = 0," and just cross out and score two cards for a total of 14 points.

When it's no longer possible for the player whose turn it is to use any of the remaining cards to form an answered addition or subtraction problem, play stops. Of course, if the next player does spot a remaining problem, he may call it out, and get credit for it. Naturally, he can do this only after his opponent gives up. Each of the players then adds up his score. High score wins.

Solitaire Version   As above, the single player crosses out as many different addition and subtraction problems with answers as he can, but in this game he is trying for low score instead of high. He wants to end up with as few cards as possible on the board since the sum of the leftover cards is his score. For example, let's say that after crossing out all possible arithmetic problems, the player is left with a 6, a 10, and a jack. He adds up the three numbers and his final score is 27. Zero (no remaining cards) is a perfect score.

Strategy   Players should plan as they play so they can come as close as possible to using up all the cards. It's best to use up the higher point cards as soon as possible so you won't be stuck with them at the end of the game.

Rank Order

Number of players   2 or more

Suggested age   9 and up

Time   15 to 20 minutes

Object   To put 3 or more cards in rank order from lowest to highest or from highest to lowest in each of the 5 horizontal, 5 vertical, and 2 diagonal rows

Materials Notebook and felt pen for each player, standard deck of playing cards, and 2 paper bags

Preparation Draw a 5 × 5 square into one of the player's notebooks (see the first diagram of this chapter). Shuffle a deck of playing cards and place them in one of your paper bags (save the other bag for discards).

In the rules which follow, the lowest card is an ace and the highest is a king. Only the *numbers* of cards are recorded in the boxes of the 5 × 5 square, not the suits. For convenience, write J for jack, Q for queen, K for king, and A for ace.

Rules One of the players picks a card from the bag, records the number in any one of the 25 boxes, and then discards it in the second bag. The next player does the same with a second card, and play continues in this manner. Players should keep in mind that the object of the game is to put three cards or more in rank order in any one of the five horizontal, five vertical, or two diagonal rows. The order can be from low to high (for example, 2, 5, 10) or from high to low (K, 6, 4). A card of *equal* value can be repeated in any one row, without spoiling the sequence. For instance, 2, 5, 5, 7 is a valid series of four.

Let's say that the playing board looks like the one shown here when the next player up picks a 10. This player will be able to complete a sequence of three cards in rank order by writing his 10 in any one of the starred squares. He then records a score of 3 (for three cards in order) in his notebook. If a player completes a sequence of four cards, he receives a score of 4, and if he completes one of five cards, he gets a score of 5.

It's possible for the same player (or different players) to score more than once in the same row. For example, if the player cited above puts his 10 below the 4 and 8 *vertically* (gray box) and the next player picks a jack (or another 10 or a queen), he writes it below the 10 and scores 5 points for a five-card sequence from low to high.

In placing a card, a player may complete more than one sequence. For example, let's say the playing board looks like the one here. If

Q	8			
4	*	9		
	5	10		

the next player up picks a 6, 7, or 8 and places it in the starred box, he completes *two* three-card sequences—a vertical one from high to low (8, 6, 5) and a horizontal one from low to high (4, 6, 9). The diagonal series (Q, 6, 10) doesn't score any points. This player records a score of 6 for the turn.

Play continues until all the boxes have been filled. Players record a score every time they complete an ordered sequence of three or more cards. At the end of the game, each player adds up his scores, and the one with the highest total wins.

Solitaire Version The single player sets up the game in the way described above. He picks one card at a time, records it in any box, and tries to form sequences of three cards or more in rank order (high-low or low-high) in each horizontal, vertical, and diagonal row. *Unlike* the standard version, he does not record scores as he goes along, but, rather, he records them when all the boxes have been filled. At that time he looks at the 12 rows and records one score for each line with a correct sequence. For an easier game, leave out the diagonal rows, and score only the 10 horizontal and vertical rows; in this case, high score is 50.

Strategy The player should try to place low cards (ace through 4) or high ones (10 through king) at the beginning or end of a row. Middle-range cards (5 through 9) should be placed somewhere in between. Of course, there are no hard and fast rules since it's impossible to know what cards will come up. The player should be careful to look at all rows in which a card appears, since the beginning of a horizontal row may be the middle of a vertical one (or vice versa). And, of course, those diagonal rows should be in rank order too! The diagram shows a sample game.

Sample Game of Rank Order Solitaire

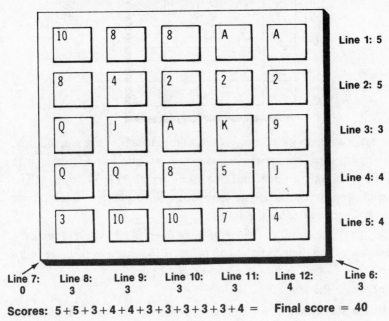

10	8	8	A	A	Line 1: 5
8	4	2	2	2	Line 2: 5
Q	J	A	K	9	Line 3: 3
Q	Q	8	5	J	Line 4: 4
3	10	10	7	4	Line 5: 4

Line 7: 0   Line 8: 3   Line 9: 3   Line 10: 3   Line 11: 3   Line 12: 4   Line 6: 3

Scores: 5 + 5 + 3 + 4 + 4 + 3 + 3 + 3 + 3 + 3 + 4 =   **Final score = 40**

When the player has totaled his score, he may want to check this chart to see how well he did:

Under 15: Poor
15 to 20: Fair
21 to 30: Good
31 to 40: Very good
41 to 50: Excellent
51 to 60: Expert!

In the games that follow, you'll have to set out many cards and move them around. To play them conveniently in a car, you can make a playing card board which can be used to play any of the games in this chapter. The board takes about 30 minutes to make, but you'll find it worth the effort for the hours of fun it brings.

How to Make a Playing Card Board To make a playing card board, you'll need a 14″ × 18″ piece of cardboard (you can cut down a side of a cardboard carton), 13 white letter envelopes (6½″ × 3½″), scissors, and cellophane tape.

1. Cut the top flap off the 13 envelopes (see the illustration on pages 160 and 161).

2. Cut each envelope in half (across the width) so you have two pieces that are closed on two sides. You now have 26 half envelopes. You'll need only 25 for your playing board.

3. Hold one of the half envelopes so that the *two closed ends* are on the *bottom* and *right* sides. Now take a playing card from a standard-sized deck, and slip it into the envelope so that the *right* edge of the card is resting snugly against the right (closed) edge of the envelope.

4. Take a scissors and *trim* the half envelope to the card width.

5. Take the card out and trim about one inch off the open top of the envelope. You are left with a card pocket that is closed on two sides. If you slip a playing card back into the pocket, you will see that the top portion of the card sticks out about one inch from the top of the pocket so that you can easily read what the card says. Make 25 card pockets in the same manner.

6. Hold the sheet of cardboard lengthwise, and place five of the card pockets in a line along the bottom edge of the cardboard (with the *closed* ends on the bottom and right sides). There will be little space between the pockets. Use cellophane tape to tape down each of the five pockets on the *bottom and right sides only.*

7. Slip a playing card into each of the five taped-down pockets so you will know how much space to leave before taping down your next row of five pockets. The next row should begin at the top of the playing cards.

8. Repeat steps 6 and 7 until you have taped down five rows of

five pockets (25 pockets in all). The top row of five pockets will probably reach the top border of the cardboard. Your completed playing board should look like the illustration.

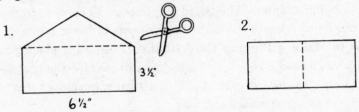

1. Cut on the dotted line (do this with 13 envelopes).
2. Cut each envelope in half as shown by the dotted line.
3. The solid lines are the closed edges of the half envelope. The dotted lines are the open edges. A card is placed in the envelope.
4. The portion with slanted lines has been trimmed, so the pocket is the same width as the playing card (do this with 25 pockets).
5. One inch is cut off the top of each pocket so you can see the card.

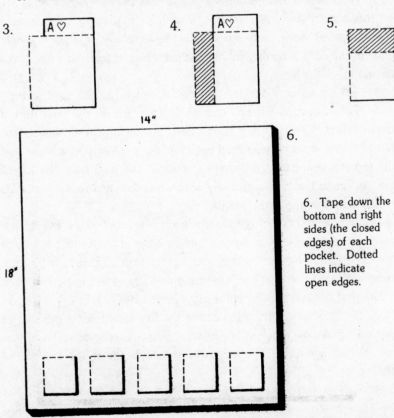

6. Tape down the bottom and right sides (the closed edges) of each pocket. Dotted lines indicate open edges.

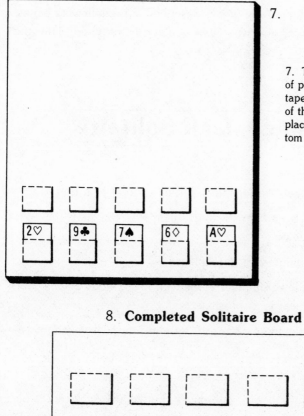

7.

7. The second row of pockets is taped at the top of the cards placed in the bottom row,

8. **Completed Solitaire Board**

When you play any of the games described in the following pages, simply slip 25 cards (or whatever number is required) into the pockets.

Jumping Jack Solitaire

Number of players   Any number, but one player at a time

Suggested age   8 and up (6- and 7-year-olds can play the easy variation which follows)

Time   10 to 15 minutes for each player

Object   To jump lower-number cards with higher-number ones and be left with as few cards as possible

Materials   One playing card board, standard deck of playing cards

Preparation   Make a playing card board following the instructions at the beginning of this section

Rules   To set up the board, the player shuffles the deck, takes the top 24 cards (face down), and one at a time, turns each one over and places it in the pocket of his choice. Twenty-four of the 25 pockets will be filled. The *center pocket* (the third pocket in the third row) is left empty.

As you will later see, it is best, if possible, to place cards with a face value of 8 or more in the outer 16 pockets and those with a face value of 7 or less in the inner 8 pockets (see illustration). Of course, this is only a suggestion, not a hard and fast rule.

Aces have a value of 1, 2's through 10's have their face value, jacks have a value of 11, queens, 12, and kings, 13.

The player moves by taking one of the cards out of its pocket, jumping over a card of *lesser* numerical value, and *removing* the card that was jumped. For example, the 10 shown in the illustration can jump over the 2 and be placed in the empty center pocket (the 2 is

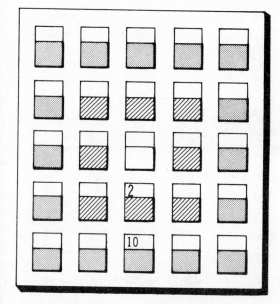

In laying out your cards, try to place those with a face value of 8 or more in the outer pockets and those with a value of 7 or less in the inner pockets. Leave the center pocket empty.

then removed from the board). A card can jump over one card on any of its four sides, as long as there is an *empty* pocket next to (and in line with) the card it is jumping over. Diagonal jumps are not allowed. As mentioned above, the face value of each card determines the cards it can jump over. For example, a king can jump a queen since it has a higher value than a queen (it can also jump any other card on the board), a queen can jump a jack (or any other card except a king) and so on, all the way down to the lowest card, ace, which has a value of one and can't jump anything except another ace (identical value cards *are* allowed to jump one another). In all cases, the card that was jumped is removed from the board. Naturally, as the game progresses, there are more and more empty pockets. The player should try to look ahead to see if any one move will set him up for others or damage his position.

When a player can no longer make a move, either because the remaining cards are not adjacent to each other or because it is not possible to jump a higher card over one of equal or lower value, play stops. The player counts the remaining cards and records that number as his score. Naturally, the lower the score, the better. One remaining card is a perfect score. If there is more than one player, the cards are removed and shuffled, and each player takes a turn at the game. The player who gets the *lowest* score wins. The single player will enjoy trying to improve his own record.

VARIATION

Mystery Score Jumping Jack (ages 6 and up)

Number of players Any number, but one player at a time

Time 10 to 15 minutes for each player

Object To jump as many "mystery" score cards as possible and be left with the lowest score

Materials One playing card board, standard deck of playing cards

Rules After shuffling the deck, the player takes the top 24 cards and, one at a time, places them *face down* in each of 24 pockets. As in the standard version, he leaves the *center* pocket (the third pocket in the third row) empty. He begins by taking one of the outer 16 cards out of its pocket and jumping over an inner card into the empty center pocket. He removes the card that was jumped. Next, he makes another jump over a card and into the empty pocket that is next to (and in line with) the card he jumped. In all cases, the card that is jumped is removed from the board. The player continues jumping cards and trying to look ahead to set himself up for more jumps. When the player can't make any more jumps, he reveals his score (this is the part of the game that my children like best). He turns over the cards that are left on the board and adds them up. Aces count for one point, 2's through 10's at face value, and all picture cards for 10 points. Naturally, the lower his score is, the better.

If more than one person is playing the game, the cards are taken out and reshuffled, and the other players take a turn at the board. The player who can turn up the *lowest total* wins. If there is only one player, he can try again for a lower score.

Three Sinister Sisters

Number of players 2 or more

Suggested age 5 and up

Time 15 to 20 minutes

Object To match and capture as many pairs as possible without turning over one of the 3 Sinister Sisters (queens)

Materials Playing card board and standard deck of playing cards

Preparation Take out these 25 cards from a standard deck (the suit of the cards doesn't matter): two aces, two 2's, two 3's, two 4's, two 5's, two 6's, two 7's, two 8's, two 9's, two 10's, two jacks, and three queens. These are the only cards you'll need to play this game. Shuffle them well, and put the other cards aside.

In the explanations which follow, pairs of aces are worth one point, pairs of 2's through 10's are worth face value, pairs of jacks are 11 points, and each queen is −5 points.

Rules To set up the game, one of the players slips each of the 25 cards *face down* into the 25 pockets. The youngest player goes first by turning over any two cards he wishes. If they're a match, he may take them off the board and record a score of 1 to 11, depending on the pair. If a player makes a match, he goes again. However, if he doesn't, he turns both cards face down again, and the next player takes his turn.

Any time a player turns over a Sinister Sister (one of the queens) he deducts 5 points from his score. If he picks a queen as his first card, he doesn't turn over a second card. Queens are *never* removed from the board. They are simply turned face down again in place. Of course, players must try to remember the position of the cards so they can make matches and avoid the three Sinister Sisters.

When all of the pairs have been captured and only the Sisters remain on the board, players add the scores of the pairs they've collected. For each time they uncovered a Sinister Sister, they must subtract 5 points from their score. High score wins.

Solitaire Version   In this game, each pair that is turned up is worth *one* point, regardless of its number.

Rules   As before, to set up the game, the player slips each of his 25 cards *face down* into the 25 pockets.   The object of the game is to match as many of the pairs from ace to jack as he can *before* turning over the three Sinister Sisters (the three queens).   He begins by turning over any two cards.   If they match, he leaves them showing. If they're different, he turns them both face down before picking two new cards.   Any time he turns over a Sinister Sister, it is *left* showing, and he continues making matches.   If his memory is good (and if he's lucky), he may match all 11 pairs before the three Sisters appear.   In this case, he wins the game with a perfect score of 11 matches. However, if all three Sisters are uncovered first, he must stop playing. He receives one point for each pair he has turned over.

VARIATION

If children over six are playing the solitaire version, they may enjoy this scoring variation.   Score 5 points for each pair turned over before the *first* Sister appears, 3 points for each pair turned over before the *second* Sister appears, and 1 point for each pair turned over before the *third* Sister appears.   When all the Sisters have been exposed, add the three scores.   The player with the highest score wins.

If you've taken the time to make a playing card board, you'll probably want to use it in place of a 5 × 5 square for the first four games of this chapter.   Just place the playing cards on the board instead of writing the numbers in squares.   In the game It All Adds Up to Fun! (page 154) simply remove the cards from the board when you make addition and subtraction problems.

Materials

1. Spiral notebook for each player
2. Felt pen or crayon for each player
3. Standard deck of playing cards
4. Two paper bags
5. Playing card board (14″ × 18″ piece of cardboard, 13 white 6½″ × 3½″ letter envelopes, scissors, cellophane tape)

BACKSEAT
7·BBG
BOARD GAMES

Expecting to take a longer car trip than usual? Pack along a few board games, and you'll wonder how you ever made it to your destination so quickly! In the games ahead, you'll be scoring touchdowns, entering cross-country races, gambling in Las Vegas, and even proving you're a Hollywood star—all without leaving your car. The games have been adapted for travel so you can enjoy them without hassle or inconvenience. If you like, you can photocopy the game paths you want to use before your trip, so you won't have to draw them. Try one on your next trip and turn each mile into a smile.

License Letters

(moderate traffic)

Suggested age 5 and up

Time 20 to 35 minutes

Object To be the first player to get from home base to your destination by following the winding path

Materials Game path in one of the player's notebooks, different color felt pen or crayon for each player, bag of commercial letter tiles (or letter slips), spinner or die in clear glass jar, watch with a second hand or two-minute egg timer

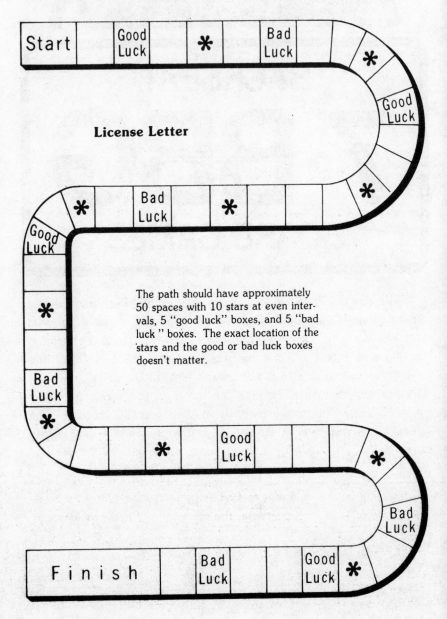

License Letter

The path should have approximately 50 spaces with 10 stars at even intervals, 5 "good luck" boxes, and 5 "bad luck" boxes. The exact location of the stars and the good or bad luck boxes doesn't matter.

Preparation   Copy the game path into one of the player's note-books. If you don't own letter tiles, take 26 slips of paper and write one letter of the alphabet on each one. Place all the slips or letter tiles into a paper bag.

Rules   Choose which player will go first. The first player spins the spinner or shoots the die and moves along the game sheet by drawing a line of his color in each box along the path beginning at start. For instance, if the player spins a 3, he draws a vertical line in each of the first 3 boxes. If he lands in a blank box, his turn is over and the next player goes. If he lands in a "good luck" box, he takes an extra turn. If he lands in a "bad luck" box, he loses his next turn. If he lands on a star he plays the alphabet quiz.

To play the alphabet quiz, a player picks a letter tile or slip and has two minutes to find that letter on as many passing license plates as he can. He moves ahead one box for each plate that he spots. For example, if the player picks the letter L and finds four license plates with an L, he puts a colored line in four consecutive boxes. If he can't find *any* cars with that letter on the plate within two minutes, he loses his next turn. (Note that letter tiles or slips are returned to the bag after the player's turn.) The first player to reach the end of his path by exact count wins the game.

VARIATION

License Numbers

This game is played like the standard version except that you use 10 number slips instead of letters. Write the digits from 0 to 9 on 10 slips, and place them in a paper bag.

If a child lands on a star, he picks a *number* slip. Let's say he picks an 8. He has two minutes to find as many license plates as he can with the number 8. Otherwise, the rules are the same as above.

Adaptation for one player   Draw 12 stars along the game path at even intervals (instead of ten stars), but do not write "good luck" or "bad luck" in any of the boxes. The object of the game is to get from start to finish, by exact count, in nine turns or less. The player spins and moves along the path. If he lands on a star, he takes the alphabet or number quiz. He can keep track of his time for the quiz with an egg timer. He should also mark down how many turns he takes. If he finishes the path in nine turns or less, he wins the game.

Capture the Color

(moderate traffic)

Suggested age 4 and up

Time 20 to 35 minutes

Object To capture as many colors as possible and be the first player to reach the rainbow

Materials One game path, one different colored crayon or felt pen for each player, spinner or die, watch with second hand or one-minute egg timer

Preparation Copy the game path into one of the player's notebooks. The path should have 60 boxes, as in the illustration, and the sequence of boxes should be red, yellow, free, free, blue, white, free, free, green, brown, free, free. (If you prefer, you can simply write an F to indicate free spaces.) This sequence is repeated until you reach the end of the path.

Rules Choose to see who will go first. The first player spins and, beginning with start, moves the required number of spaces by putting a line of his color through each box as he passes through it. If he lands on a free space, his turn is over and the next player goes. However, if he lands on a color—let's say red—he has the opportunity to capture that color. To do this he must spin again. Let's suppose he spins a 5. He has exactly one minute to point out five different red cars on the road. If he fails, nothing happens, and red is still an uncaptured color. If he succeeds, he writes his name in each red space along the path. From then on, whenever another player

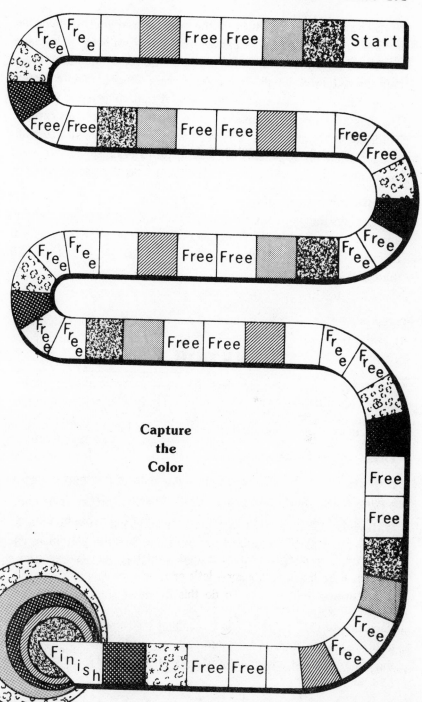

Start

Free Free

Free Free

Free Free

Free Free

Free

Free

Free Free

Free Free

Free

Free

Free Free

**Capture
the
Color**

Free

Free

Free

Free

Finish Free Free

lands on red, he loses his turn. If the owner of red lands on that color in future moves, he gets an extra turn. Play continues. If a player lands on a color that hasn't been captured, he spins a number, tries to find the required number of colored cars in one minute and, if successful, writes his name in each box of that color along the path. There is no limit on the number of colors one player can capture. Naturally, the more colors a player "owns," the more extra turns he will get, while his opponents will lose turns. The first player to reach the rainbow (the finish box) by exact count wins the game.

Adaptation for one player Draw the same game path. The single player plays the game the same way as above, but he ignores the rule about taking extra turns. The object of the game is for the player to capture *all* the colors, by the time he has reached the end of the path (by exact count).

Hollywood Stars

(moderate traffic)

Suggested age 4 and up (the banker should be at least 7 years old)

Time 20 to 35 minutes

Object To be the Hollywood star who collects the most money by waving at his "fans" and getting them to wave back

Materials Game path in each player's notebook, one crayon or felt pen for each player, spinner (1 to 6) or die, $100 in play money for each player (plus extra play money for the bank), one-minute egg timer or watch with second hand

Preparation Draw a square game path in each player's notebook. Each side of the square should have eight boxes, and there should be a total of seven stars at even intervals around the path. Each side of the square should have one note to *get* money and one note to *give back* money.

Start		You get $50	★		Give back $30		★
Give back $80							
★			Hollywood Stars!				Give back $10
You get $70							You get $20
★	Give back $60		★		You get $100		★

Make a pack of Lucky Bucks in the denominations stated here or use play money from a commercial game. You'll need 30 $10 bills, 20 $50 bills and 20 $100 bills. Use a different color for each denomination to avoid confusion. Each player needs $100 to begin the game (one $50 and five $10 bills). You may want to put each player's money into a plain white envelope to keep it together. The balance of the money can be kept in a larger envelope or, better yet, a shoebox. (See the variation below for a version of this game played with poker chips.)

Rules Choose one player (or adult) to be the banker. The highest spin or throw of the die goes first. The first player spins the spinner and moves the number of spaces indicated by drawing a diagonal line through each box he enters, beginning with start. If he lands on a box that says he gets money, the banker gives him the correct amount. If he lands on a box that tells him to give back money, he gives the banker the correct amount. If he doesn't have enough, he hands over whatever he has and loses his next turn. Whenever a player lands on a star, he gets to test his "fame." He has one minute to wave to all his "fans" in the passing cars. Every time a fan waves back, it's worth $10 (the player keeps score out loud as he keeps waving to *different* people). At the end of a minute, the player collects his $10 for each different fan that waved back at him. For example, if 10 fans waved back, he gets $100. His turn is now over, and the next player goes. In this way all players go around their game paths *twice*. The second time around, the player draws a second diagonal line in each box to complete the letter X, as shown here. Every player gets to go around his game path twice, ending in the start box (exact count is *not* necessary). It makes no difference who finishes first. When all players have gone around twice, the richest player wins the game.

Adaptation for one player   The object of the game for one player is to accumulate $500 to take a trip to Hollywood. He starts out with $100 and moves around the board in the same manner as in the standard game—giving back money when required to, getting money when indicated, and playing the waving game when he lands on a star (he should use an egg timer so he can keep track of time for himself). After two trips around the board, he wins the game if he has collected enough money to go to Hollywood.

Note   If traffic is thin, allow three trips around the board.

VARIATION

If you don't have play money and prefer not to make any, use red and white poker chips instead. Reds count for 10 points, and whites for 1. Each person starts with 10 white chips, stored in a jar or plastic container. Altogether you will need about 50 white chips and 30 reds. Whenever the supply of white chips runs low, 10 of them can be traded in for one red one. In the waving game the player receives one white chip for each person who waves back. The player who has accumulated the most chips after two trips around the board wins the game. To modify the board, substitute "5 chips" for "$50," "3 chips" for "$30," and so on.

Highway Football

(light traffic)

Number of players Even number (2, 4, or 6)

Suggested age 6 and up

Time 20 to 45 minutes

Object To score more touchdowns and bonus points than the opposing team

Materials One football field game picture, felt pen for each player, paper bag with category slips, watch with second hand or one-minute egg timer

Preparation Copy the football field below into one of the player's notebooks. Color one team's yard lines and goal post red, the other team's blue, and the 50-yard line half red and half blue (naturally, any two colors can be used).

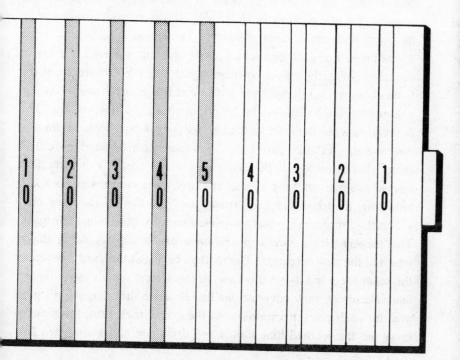

Write each of the following categories on 16 different slips of paper and put them in a paper bag:

1. Things smaller than a bicycle
2. Things larger than a car
3. Road signs
4. Natural scenery (not man-made)
5. Living things (plants or animals)
6. Man-made things
7. Stores (use only when appropriate)
8. Types of transportation
9. Wooden things
10. Metal things
11. Green things
12. White things
13. Yellow things
14. Brown things
15. Black things
16. Red things

You can choose any categories which require children to observe something in the scenery. However, there should be an even number of slips so that each team gets an equal number of turns.

Rules Draw a small football above the 50-yard line. The teams choose to see who will get the ball first (see Chapter 1, page 5, for new ways to choose for first). The first team up picks a slip from the bag and has one minute to point out as many things as possible in the scenery that fit the category on the slip. If two or three people are on the team, they can all call out objects. The opposing team or an adult keeps time. For each correct response, the ball is moved one line in the direction of the opposing team's goal post. For example, if the team chooses "red things" and finds three things which are red within one minute, the ball moves to the opposing team's 20-yard line. The team crosses out the little football above the 50-yard line and draws a new one above the 20-yard line. No response can be used more than once. For example, if the team gets a red car, it can't use that answer again, even if the players spot five more red cars on the road. However, they can say "red truck" or "red bus" if they see one. When the first team up has completed its turn, the other team goes. The players pick a new slip and have one minute to name things which fit the new category. The football begins at the yard line where the other team left it—in this case, at the second team's own 20-yard line. Naturally, they advance one line closer to their opponent's goal post for each correct response. At the end of their turn, the players cross out the football that stands and draw one above the yard line they've moved to. If either team gives enough correct responses to move all the way to the opposing goal post, it scores a touchdown (2 points). If the team gives *more* than the required number of responses for a touchdown within the time limit, it receives one bonus point for *every* extra correct answer. For example, if a team begins at the 50-yard line and names eight correct items, it receives a total of 5 points—2 points for the touchdown (the first five answers), and 3 points for the three extra correct answers. Whenever a team makes a touchdown, the ball is moved back to the 50-yard line before the opposing team is up. Teams alternate picking slips from the bag until there are none left (used slips should not be returned to the bag). When all the slips are used up, the team that has scored the most points wins the game.

Adaptation for one player You'll need only eight category slips for a one-person game. In addition to the materials above, you'll need a pair of dice. The player chooses a category slip and has one minute to find as many things in the scenery as he can which fit the category. He should use an egg timer to keep track of his own time. Then he crosses out the football above the 50-yard line and moves it one line closer to the Phantom's goal for each correct item he names. When his turn is over, he shoots the dice to see how well the Phantom scores. He moves the ball for the Phantom the number of yard lines shown on the dice toward his own goal post. If the Phantom's ball reaches the goal post, it scores a touchdown (2 points) plus one bonus point for each dot on the dice exceeding the number needed for the touchdown. The player alternates with the Phantom. When both have had eight turns, their scores are totaled. Who will win—the player or the Phantom?

Checker and SCRABBLE® Crossword Games

In recent years, as families have become more mobile, so have many of the more popular board games. Magnetic sets of chess, checkers, and backgammon as well as the special travel edition of the SCRABBLE® Crossword Game now make it possible to enjoy these family favorites in a moving vehicle.* These games are fun to play without any extras or changes, but here are a few variations for the adventurous (or restless) among you.

*SCRABBLE® is the registered trademark of Selchow & Righter Company for a line of crossword and sentence games.

You're Sandwiched!

Number of players 2 (all checker games in this section require 2 players)

Suggested age 7 and up

Time 15 to 30 minutes

Object To use your checkers to "sandwich" your opponent's checkers and capture all but one of his pieces

Materials Magnetic checker set

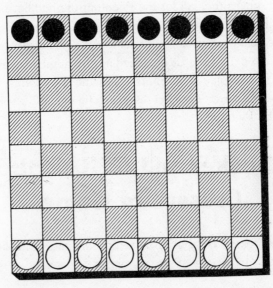

Rules To play this game, each player will need only 8 checkers. Players should line up their checkers across the entire horizontal row closest to them (see the illustration on page 178).

The first player takes any one of his checkers and moves it *any number* of boxes—vertically, diagonally, and, in later moves, horizontally—in *one straight line*. Now the next player moves by doing the same thing. Both players try to set up the board so that they will be in a position to sandwich their opponent horizontally, vertically, or diagonally and thus remove that piece from the board. For example,

let's say the board looks like the one below. The black player and the red player have both moved once. It's now black's move again. There are two ways he can sandwich red's checker. He can either move the checker with the X on it three boxes *vertically* or the checker with the Y on it three boxes *diagonally*. He then says, "You're sandwiched!" and removes the red checker from the board.

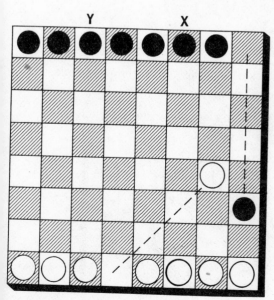

The dotted lines indicate the starting positions and paths taken by these two checkers.

Players continue taking turns in this way—trying to remove their opponent's pieces by sandwiching them and avoiding moves that will land them in the center of the opponent's sandwich!

Players are permitted to make "double decker" or even "triple decker" sandwiches by sandwiching in two or three of an opponent's checkers, if such an opportunity arises. Double deckers and triple deckers look like these:

Naturally, vertical or diagonal double or triple deckers are also allowed. In either of these cases, the player removes *all* of his opponent's sandwiched checkers.

When one player has only one checker left, he can no longer make sandwiches, and his opponent wins the game.

Your Time Is Running Out!

Suggested age 6 and up

Time 15 to 25 minutes

Object To race to your finish line in the shortest time

Materials Magnetic checker set, pair of dice in a clear glass jar, notebook, and felt pen for each player

Preparation Players draw a clock face in their notebooks, as shown, and set the time at 11 o'clock

Rules The runners in this race start from opposite ends of the field at 11:00 A.M., as shown on their clocks. Each runner puts one checker of his color in the lower left-hand corner of his side of the board (players will need only one checker). See the diagram for the route the players take to get from the starting position to the finish line. The squares with the X's are the hills and valleys. The route finishes in the player's lower right-hand corner (it looks the same from either side of the board). The black squares are safe, and the red ones are penalties. The first player shoots the dice and moves his piece. If he lands on a black square, he's safe, and the other player goes. If he lands on a red, however, he must move his clock ahead five minutes by drawing a new minute hand, but *not* filling it in.

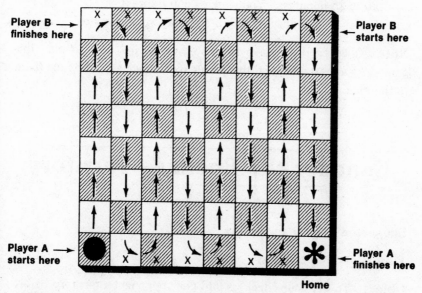

Player B finishes here

Player B starts here

Player A starts here

Player A finishes here

Home

Whenever a player lands on a hill or valley (the squares with X's), he must shoot a double on his next turn. If he doesn't roll a double, he must stay where he is, move the minute hand of his clock ahead five minutes, and try for a double again on his next turn. If he does not get a double after three tries (a time loss of 15 minutes), he may continue to move ahead on his fourth turn.

If a player has moved completely around the clock (one full hour), he fills in the minute hand on the second time. When one player reaches the end of his path—exact count is not necessary—he waits for the other to finish. A player does not lose five minutes if his finish square happens to be red. It doesn't matter who finishes first. The winner is the player who arrives home the earliest. My seven-year-old son's best time was an 11:25 arrival.

Adaptation for one player The single player should go from start to finish, following the same rules. He can then look at this rating scale to see how well he did:

Hour or more: You must have napped on the way
50 to 55 minutes: Just made it!
40 to 45 minutes: Your nickname is "Limber Legs"
30 to 35 minutes: You'll have time for a sandwich!
20 to 25 minutes: You're the Pony Express!
Under 20 minutes: You're a space-age phenomenon!

Note Children don't have to know how to tell time to play this game. As a matter of fact, this is an excellent way to introduce them to the idea.

Conquer the Enemy's Territory

Suggested age 9 and up

Time 20 to 40 minutes

Object To get your checkers into your opponent's territory before he can get his checkers into yours and to capture as many of your opponent's pieces as you can

Materials Magnetic checker set, standard deck of playing cards, discard bag for used cards

Preparation Remove the 7's, 8's, 9's, and 10's of all suits from your deck of cards since you won't need them. Shuffle the remaining cards well, and hold them together with a loose rubber band.

Rules Each player should set up his twelve checkers as shown in the illustration. The first row of checkers begins at the player's left-hand corner and stops two boxes from the right end. The second row of checkers starts at the right and stops two boxes from the left end. The two full rows of boxes closest to you, those that contain your checkers, are your territory. The two full rows that contain your opponent's checkers are his territory.

One of the players turns over the top card of the deck. If the card is *black* (either a club or a spade), the "instructions" on the card apply to the player with the black checkers. If the card is *red* (either a diamond or a heart), the "instructions" on the card apply to the player with the red checkers. (If the two colors of your checkers are *not* red and black, you will have to decide in advance which player will follow which color cards.) Instructions for the cards are given here:

Ace: The player moves any one of his men *one space* in any direction—horizontally, vertically, or diagonally (forward or backward).

2 through 6: The player moves any one of his men the number of spaces indicated on the card. As with an ace, the piece

can move in any direction, as long as it moves in one straight line. The checker is *not* allowed to jump over a piece which is in its way. If it is impossible for the player to make the indicated move because there are no clear, straight paths of that many boxes, the player forfeits his turn.

Jack: The player *loses* his next turn. This means that the next time a card of *his* color is turned over, his must pass it up.

Queen: One of the player's checkers may *switch places* with any of his opponent's men.

King: The player may move any one of his checkers into *any* unoccupied space on the board.

To jump an opponent, a player moves into a box which contains one of his opponent's checkers. For example, let's say the game has just begun and a red 5 is turned up. The red player may move any one of his men ahead five spaces into a box containing a black checker. Then he removes the black checker from the board (see the illustration).

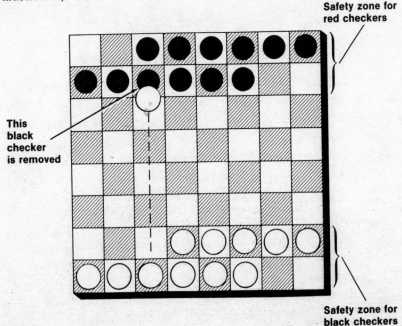

Safety zone for red checkers

This black checker is removed

Safety zone for black checkers

Naturally, a jump can be made only by exact count. As a result of the jump illustrated, one of red's checkers is now in his opponent's territory. However, the opponent's territory (those last two horizontal rows) is a *safety zone* for red's pieces. In other words, once a red checker has made it to that territory, it cannot be jumped. For example, using the same illustration, if the next card turned up is a black ace, one of the black checkers surrounding that red piece *cannot* move in and jump it. However, if the next card is a red ace, the red checker *can* move in and jump any one of the black pieces adjacent to it. Naturally, red's territory is a safety zone for black. (Red checkers cannot jump black ones in red territory, but blacks can jump red checkers there.)

One by one the cards are turned up, and the players follow the directions indicated by the card. A player may sometimes get as many as four or five turns in a row if his color cards keep coming up, but things will even out as you go through the deck. The player who is up should keep two goals in mind: first, to move his men into his opponent's two-row territory and, second, to remove his opponent's checkers from the board by landing in boxes that his opponent occupies.

Sometimes, a player may be forced to move one of his pieces out of his safety zone (on his opponent's side of the board). For example, let's say one of the players turns up a 6, and the only piece that can move six spaces is one of his checkers in his safety zone. The player *must* move it. Of course, once that piece is out of the safety zone, it can be jumped.

Once a card has been used, put it in the discard bag. When players have gone through the entire deck, they take all the used cards, reshuffle them, and use them again. The game stops when one of the players has gotten *all* of his remaining pieces into his opponent's territory. Then points are scored as follows: 5 points go to the player who is *first* to get all of his remaining pieces into the opponent's territory. Both players score 2 points for *each* checker they captured from their opponent. The player who scores the most points wins the game.

Category Crossword

Suggested age 9 and up

Time About an hour and 15 minutes

Object To earn bonus points by forming words which belong to a chosen category

Materials Travel edition of the SCRABBLE® Crossword Game, felt pen and notebook to keep score

Rules This game is played exactly like the regular SCRABBLE® Crossword Game except that the players agree on a bonus category before picking their first set of letters. If children under 10 are playing, the bonus category should be a very broad one, such as "foods" (any kind of food or drink), "living things" (plants or animals), "household items" (furniture, clothing, utensils), and so on. If the players are all 10 or over, you can pick something more specific, like "fruits and vegetables," "colors," "articles of clothing," and so on. (See Chapter 3, You're on TV! page 69 , for category ideas.) If children eight or under are playing with older children or adults, spot them 25 to 100 points to even up the game.

Whenever a player makes a word which fits the bonus category, he receives a bonus of 25 points in addition to his regular score for the word. This holds true only for the person who puts down the word—not for a player who adds to it. If a player can put down a seven-letter word which fits the bonus category, he receives the usual 50-point bonus for using up all his letter tiles plus the 25-point category bonus. Naturally, the player with the highest score wins.

Take a Giant Step

Suggested age 8 and up

Time 30 to 45 minutes

Object To earn the highest total score by using all your 14 letters to form crossword patterns

Materials Special travel edition of the SCRABBLE* Crossword Game, felt pen and notebook to keep score, watch with second hand or two-minute egg timer

Rules The youngest child goes first, and the others follow in order of age. That first player picks 14 letter tiles to fill two racks. At the starting signal, he begins on the center star of the game board and uses as many of his 14 letters as he can to form words in a crossword pattern. For example, he may use his 14 letters to form the following words:

```
                    R
                    A   I  R
            J       V
        Q   U   I   E   T
            T       N
                    S
```

All of his words must be connected to one another as in a regular game. At the end of two minutes, time is called, and the player must stop, even if he hasn't finished. He scores his words (including double-word scores, double-letter scores, and so on) just like a regular game. After he adds his individual word scores, he *subtracts* the point value of the letters he didn't use. For example, if the player's total score is 56 and he's left with a C (3 points) and a U (1 point), he subtracts 4 points and is left with a score of 52. If the player was able to use up all of his 14 letter tiles, he receives a bonus of 25 points. If any of the player's words has seven letters or more, that word is scored with a bonus of 50 points. In the rare case that the player makes and connects two seven-letter words, he receives a 100-point bonus, plus 25 more points for using up all 14 tiles.

If the player doesn't use up all of his 14 tiles, he puts the unused tiles back in the box or bag, and his turn is over. The next player picks 14 tiles and uses them to form a crossword pattern which is connected in *at least one place* with the crossword pattern made by the first player. For example, the second player may connect to the first crossword pattern in just one place, as in the first diagram (using the S in "ravens"), or in more than one place, as in the second. The

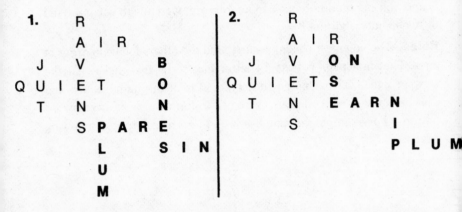

second player figures out his score counting connecting words just as in a regular game and returns his unused letters to the box or bag. Play continues. In all cases, there is a two-minute time limit, and unused letters are subtracted from the total score and returned to the bag. Naturally, as the board begins closing up, the game gets tougher. The only time a player may change his letters is when he picks either 14 vowels or 14 consonants. In these cases, he may put back *all* 14 tiles and pick 14 new ones without losing his turn. However, if he picks any combination of vowels and consonants (or a blank tile, which can stand for anything), he must do the best he can and subtract the point value of any letters he doesn't use.

When there are less than 14 letters remaining, the player picks all the letters that are left and tries to use as many of them as possible in two minutes. When he is working with less than 14 letters, he doesn't receive a 25-point bonus for using them all up, but he still subtracts points for whatever letters he doesn't use. When each player has had two chances to use the last remaining letters, the game stops. Players add up all their scores, and the one with the highest score wins.

Note If children of nine or under are playing with older players, spot them 25 to 100 points. You may also want to allow younger children more time to form words.

Spiral Word Game

Suggested age   9 and up

Time   About an hour and 15 minutes

Object   To connect your words to the last letter or letters of your opponent's words in a continuous chain and get the highest score

Materials   Travel edition of the SCRABBLE® Crossword Game, felt pen and notebook to keep score

B_3	A_1	R_1	G_2	E_1	A_1	R_1	L_1	A_1	T_1	E_1	W_4	E_1	A_1	R_1
	DOUBLE WORD SCORE			TRIPLE LETTER SCORE				TRIPLE LETTER SCORE				DOUBLE WORD SCORE		I_1
E_1	L_1	M_3	O_1	O_1	N_1	E_1	X_8	T_1	R_1	I_1	P_3	U_1	DOUBLE WORD SCORE	D_2
Y_4		DOUBLE WORD SCORE							DOUBLE WORD SCORE			N_1		S_1
N_1			DOUBLE WORD SCORE						DOUBLE WORD SCORE			U_1		A_1
A_1	TRIPLE LETTER SCORE			TRIPLE LETTER SCORE				TRIPLE LETTER SCORE				T_1	TRIPLE LETTER SCORE	S_1
E_1				DOUBLE LETTER SCORE		DOUBLE LETTER SCORE						A_1		H_4
M_3							★					L_1		I_1
A_1	E_1			DOUBLE LETTER SCORE		DOUBLE LETTER SCORE						L_1		N_1
T_1	V_4			TRIPLE LETTER SCORE				TRIPLE LETTER SCORE				Y	TRIPLE LETTER SCORE	E_1
O_1	I_1		DOUBLE WORD SCORE						DOUBLE WORD SCORE			O_1		D_1
O_1	G_2	DOUBLE WORD SCORE								DOUBLE WORD SCORE		U_1		I_1
T_1	O_1	D_2	U_1	H_4	T_1	O_1	P_3	I_1	R_1	G_2	"N"			C_3
I_1	DOUBLE WORD SCORE			TRIPLE LETTER SCORE				TRIPLE LETTER SCORE				DOUBLE WORD SCORE		E_1
J_1	S_1	E_1	R_1	A_1	F_4	O_1	S_1	D_2	N_1	E_1	K_5	E_1	"E"	W_4

* This board is a copy of the SCRABBLE® Crossword Game board design© 1948 Selchow & Righter Company. Reprinted with permission.

Rules This is a good variation for players who rarely get to use "triple-word scores." As a matter of fact, this game begins on one.

Players pick seven letters for their racks. The youngest player goes first, and the others take turns in order of age. The first player must begin his word in the upper left-hand corner of the board, on the triple-word score box, and make any word of two letters or more, horizontally. The first player in the sample game made the word "barge" and scored it as it would be in a standard game. Now that player's turn is over. He picks new tiles to replace the ones he used, for he should always have seven tiles. The next player takes his turn. From this point on, the game bears little resemblance to a standard game. You'll find it helpful to refer to the sample game on page 189 as you read these rules.

The second player must begin his word with the *last* letter or letters of the first player's word and continue in a left to right direction. For example, in the sample game, the second player made the word "earl"—using the E from "barge" as his first letter; another possibility would have been using the GE from "barge" as his first two letters to make "geese," and so on. When the second player or any subsequent player scores his word, he counts every bonus square (triple-word score, double-letter score, and so on) that the letters of his word fall on—even if one of those letters was put down by a previous player. For example, after the second player made the word "earl," the next player made the word "late," starting with the L from "earl." The L of that word was on a triple-word score box, so the player who made "late" will also triple the point value of his word.

If a player can end his word in the last box of any horizontal or vertical row, he receives a bonus score of 25 points. For example, the player who made "wear" in the sample game finished off a horizontal row evenly and so scored 25 points in addition to his regular score. When the top row has been filled in from left to right, players begin working their way down the vertical column on the extreme right. If the last word in the top row ended a few boxes from the end (which in this case it did not), the player may begin his word in the horizontal row, wind around the corner, and finish his word vertically. In this case, however, he doesn't get the 25-point bonus.

There is one exception to the rule that each new word must begin with the last letter or letters of the previous player's word. If a player adds a letter to a word which *changes* it and adds a new word besides, he receives full credit for both words. For example, in the sample game, one player made the word "rid" (upper right-hand corner). The next player made the word "sash," which changed "rid" to "rids" and in addition formed a new word. This player receives credit for *both* words. The same thing happened slightly farther down the same column, when one player made the word "dice" and, by doing so, changed the previous word "shine" to "shined."

When players have come to the end of the first vertical column, they must turn to the *left* and continue across the bottom row from right to left. (Movement in this game is always in a clockwise direction.) Of course, the words must be read backward, but that's part of the fun. It's also all right to use the entire previous word as part of your new word. For example, in the bottom right-hand corner of the sample board, one player made the word "week," and the next added "end" to form the word "weekend."

In this game it's very difficult to make a seven-letter word, so a word of seven letters or more receives a 50-point bonus, even if the player doesn't put down all seven letters himself. For example, the player who put down "end" to form the word "weekend" made a seven-letter word, even though he added only three letters. He still receives 50 points in addition to his regular score. This rule does not apply to the player who simply adds S, ED, or ING to an existing word of five, six, or more letters. Thus, the player who added the S to "weekend" and continued to make the word "sofa" received credit for both words, but *no extra bonus.* Here are some examples of word additions which would qualify for a 50-point bonus: "*whole*some," "*actions,*" "*under*stand," "*cap*able."

If a player is unable to add a word to the existing chain in any of the ways described above, he can either pass or exchange some or all of his letters for new ones. He loses his turn when he does this.

Because it's too difficult to put down a word beginning with X, players may not make words which end with X. However, the X can hold any other position in the word, as in "next," "exit," "boxes," and so on.

When players have reached the end of the bottom line, they wind around the corner and make words in the left vertical column which reads from bottom to top. That left vertical row ends two boxes short of the top of the board and then winds around and goes from left to right again. There should be a full row of boxes between the first line of words (starting with "barge") and the inner line of words (starting with "elm"). Do this at every corner of the chain.

When all the letters have been taken from the bag and players can no longer use the remaining letters in their hands to make new words, the game stops and scores are totaled. Players subtract the point value of the letters that remain in their hands. The player with the highest score wins.

Las Vegas Fortune Hunt

Suggested age   9 and up

Time   25 to 40 minutes

Object   To collect the most money in three trips around the board

Materials   Game path and felt pen for each player, one jar with a pair of dice, one jar with *one* die, $200 in play money for each player plus extra money for the bank

Preparation   Draw the game path into each player's notebook. The short sides of the rectangle should have seven squares and the long sides 11 squares.

You will need the following amounts of play money: 20 $100 bills, 10 $500 bills, 20 $50 bills, and 30 $10 bills. Either borrow it from a commercial game or make your own.

Each player begins the game with $200—one $100 bill, one $50 bill, and five $10 bills. Put each player's money in an envelope or plastic bag. Put the bank's money (all the remaining bills) in a shoebox or cigar box.

Rules   The first player shoots *one* die and, beginning at start, moves the indicated number of boxes by drawing a diagonal line through each box.

If he lands on a blank, his turn is over, and the next player goes.

If he lands on a box which says "Odds or evens," he may call a bet from $10 to $50 on either odds or evens. Let's say he calls "evens" and bets $30. He shoots *one* die. If he rolls an even number (2, 4, or 6), he wins $30 from the bank. However, if he rolls an odd number (1, 3, or 5), he must pay the bank $30. (Players don't have to bet unless they want to.)

If a player lands in a box which says "Beat your first throw," he may choose to place a bet from $10 to $50. He then shoots two dice to determine what number he must beat. Now he shoots the dice again. If he shoots a higher number on his second throw, he wins the

Start		Odd or even?	Deluxe dice game	Beat your first throw		Pay Square $100
						Beat your first throw
Odd or even?						Deluxe dice game
Beat your first throw			LAS			Odd or even?
Deluxe dice game			VEGAS			
Pay Square $100		Deluxe dice game	Beat your first throw	Odd or even?		Pay Square $100

amount of his bet from the bank. If he shoots a lower number, he must pay the bank the amount of his bet. If he rolls the same number, he doesn't win or lose money. (Again, he doesn't have to bet.)

If a player lands on a box which says "Deluxe dice game," all players may join in the betting. Each player may bet from $10 to $100 (once they call out their bets, they can't change their minds). The player shoots both dice. If he rolls a 7 or an 11, all bettors win the amount of their bets from the bank. If the player rolls a 2 or a 3, all bettors lose and must pay the bank the amount of their bets. However, if the player rolls any other number (4, 5, 6, 8, 9, 10, 12), he must continue shooting the dice in order to roll the same number again *before* a 7 appears. If he is successful, all players win the amount of their bets from the bank. However, if a 7 appears first, everyone loses and must pay the bank the amount of his bet. If the player who landed on "Deluxe dice game" doesn't want to bet, but the other players do, he plays the dice game for them but doesn't win or lose money.

If a player lands on a "Pay square," he automatically receives $100 from the bank.

If a player lands on a devil, he immediately shoots both dice three times in a row. If he rolls a double on any of his throws, he is safe. However, if he doesn't roll a double in three tries, he must pay each player $50.

Players go around the board three times, ending in the start box (exact count isn't necessary). The second time around, they draw a second diagonal line in each box to complete an X. The third time around, they fill in the whole box like this. It doesn't matter who finishes first. When all players have completed three times around, the player who has accumulated the most money wins the game.

Notes If a player loses all his money, he can't make any more bets until he gets money again, either by landing on a "Pay square" or from another player who lands on a devil (He ignores the devil squares if he is broke.)

For the last time around the board, players can bet any amount they choose. Once a player completes his three trips around the board, he cannot bet in the "Deluxe dice game."

Shoot *one* die to move around the board. Shoot two dice only for the "Deluxe dice game," "Beat your first throw," or to try for doubles after landing on the devil. If you don't want to bring along two jars you can use one shaker which contains a pair of dice and take out the second die when it isn't needed.

VARIATION

When a player lands on "Deluxe dice game," the other players can also bet *against* him. If they bet against the player who is shooting the dice and that player *wins,* they lose their money to the bank. However, if he *loses,* they win the amount of their bet from the bank.

Adaptation for one player Use the standard game path and follow the same rules for all of the boxes. The player and the Phantom each begin the game with $200 (use separate envelopes for each). Only the player will move around on the game path. Any time the player lands on a betting square ("Odds or evens," "Beat your first throw," or "Deluxe dice game") he *must* bet something if he has money (minimum, $10). If he wins his bet, he takes the appropriate amount of money from the bank. However, if he loses, he must give his money to the Phantom. If he lands on the devil and doesn't shoot a double in three tries, he must pay the Phantom $50. After three times around the board, if the player has more money than the Phantom, he wins the game.

Don't Pick the Bean!

Number of Players 2

Suggested age 4 and up

Time 10 to 20 minutes

Object To be the first player to reach the end of the game path without picking the bean

Materials One game path, different color felt pen or crayon for each player, one die or spinner, paper bag with slips, notebook

Preparation Draw the game path shown into one player's notebook. The path should have 40 boxes, five beans spaced at even intervals, five boxes which say "Extra turn," five which say "Lose a turn" and five which say "Advance to next bean."

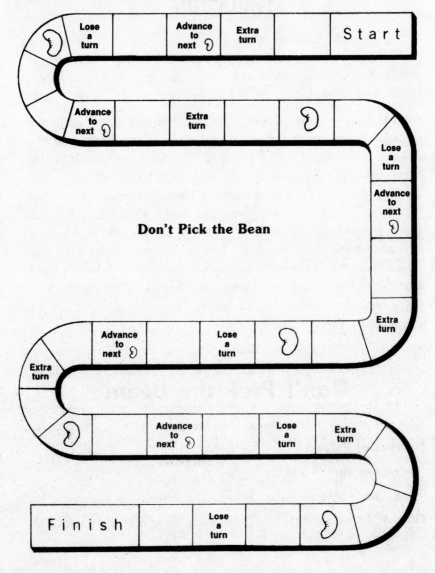

Rip a sheet of paper into 10 slips. Leave nine of the slips blank, draw a bean on one, and put all the slips into a paper bag.

Rules The first player shoots the die and moves along the game path by drawing one diagonal line of his color in each consecutive box, beginning in the start box. If the player lands in a blank box, his turn is over, and the next player goes. If he lands on a space that says "Extra turn" or "Lose a turn," he follows those directions. If he lands on a space that says "Advance to next bean," he moves along the path, drawing diagonal lines, until he arrives at the next bean. Now he must pick a slip from the "bean bag." If there's no bean drawn on it, he's safe, and the game continues as before. However, if he chooses the slip with the bean, he automatically loses the game. Whenever a player lands directly on a bean, he must also pick a slip.

The second player who starts along the game path draws a diagonal line in each box with his color pen. If there is already a line of the other person's color in the boxes that he passes, he draws his line the opposite way to form an X. Players continue taking turns. If none of the players picks the bean in the course of the game, the first one to arrive at the finish square, by exact count, wins the game.

Adaptation for more than two players If three children are playing the game, put 12 slips into the bag—10 blanks and two with beans on them. If one player picks a slip with a bean on it, he is eliminated from the game, and the remaining two players continue. If four people are playing, place 15 slips in the bag—12 blanks and three with beans. For five people, 18 slips—14 blanks and four with beans. There should always be one less bean than there are people playing. If there are more than two players, they should each have different colored felt pens or crayons and draw a vertical line of their color in each box they pass through.

Adaptation for one player On the game path for the single player, don't write "Extra turn" or "Lose a turn" in any of the boxes. Make seven boxes with beans and seven boxes which say "Advance to next bean" (put one a few boxes before each bean). The "bean bag" should have only seven slips—six blanks and one bean. The object of the game is for the player to get from start to finish without picking the bean. If he does so, he wins the game.

Double or Nothing
Letter Auto Race

Suggested age   8 and up

Time   15 to 30 minutes

Object   To be the first driver to complete a lap around the track

Materials   Game path in one player's notebook, one die in clear glass jar, bag of letter tiles or slips, watch with second hand or one-minute egg timer

Preparation   Draw the game path. There should be 40 spaces along the oval and a shortcut path of six squares, cutting across the bottom 12 squares of the oval. Write "Out of gas" in four squares along the oval and in one square on the shortcut path. Write "Full speed ahead" in four other squares on the oval and in one square along the shortcut path. Also draw seven stars at even intervals along the oval path and one star along the shortcut.

If you don't own commercial letter tiles, write the letters from A to Z on 26 separate slips of paper or 26 index cards and place them in a paper bag.

Rules   The first player shoots the die and, beginning in the start box, moves the number of spaces indicated by writing his first initial with his color felt pen or crayon, in each box he passes through. If he lands on a blank square, his turn is over, and the next player goes. If he lands on "Out of gas," he loses his next turn, and if he lands on "Full speed ahead," he may take an extra turn. Whenever he lands on a star, he gets to play the "Bonus moves letter game." To do this, he picks one letter tile or card from the bag and must say any word which contains that letter. For example, if he picks a T, he may say "bite." If he can't supply a word, his turn is over. However, if he supplies a correct word, he has a choice—he can either stop playing and move ahead *one* extra space or gamble—double or nothing —and continue. If he decides to continue, he picks a second letter

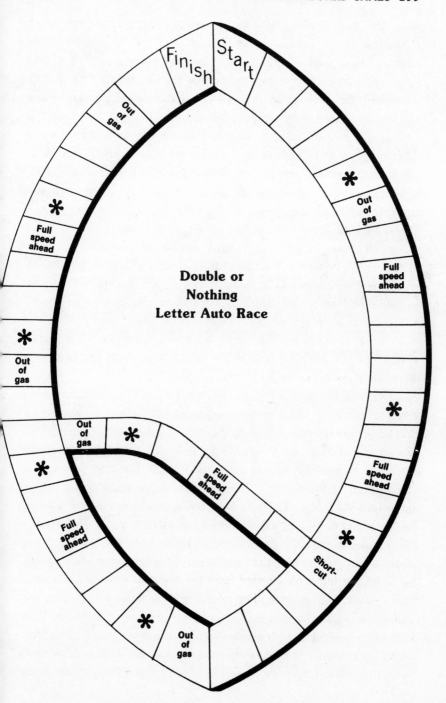

from the bag—say an R—and must now supply a word which contains both the letters T and R, such as "dirt" (the order of the letters doesn't matter). If he can't supply a word with these two letters, he stays where he is, and his turn is over. But if he's successful, he has a choice again—either to stop playing and move ahead two spaces or to continue gambling for four spaces (double or nothing). If he continues, he now picks a third letter—say, W—and must supply a word which contains all three letters—R, T, and W (in any order), such as "throw." As before, his turn is over if he misses. If he's successful, he has the choice of moving ahead four spaces or trying for a fourth letter to move ahead eight spaces or none. A word containing five letters the player picked would allow him to move ahead 16 spaces (this is the maximum number of spaces he can move in one turn). Naturally, each time the player decides to continue, he risks losing all the bonus squares he has won. Players have a one-minute time limit for thinking of a word which contains the necessary letters (younger players can be given *two* minutes).

If a player lands on "Shortcut" he may cut across the oval and save some moves. The first player to reach or cross the finish line wins the game (exact count isn't necessary).

Adaptation for one player The single player alternates taking turns for himself and a Phantom opponent. He moves by writing his first initial in each box he passes through and moves the Phantom by writing a P in each box the Phantom passes through. The rules are the same as above with one exception—if the Phantom lands on a star instead of playing the "Bonus moves letter game," the player shoots the die for him to figure out his bonus moves. If he shoots an *odd* number (1, 3, or 5), the Phantom stays where he is. However, if the number is *even* (2, 4, or 6) the Phantom wins one bonus space, and the player must shoot for him again. Two even throws in a row, the Phantom moves ahead two spaces; three even throws in a row, four spaces; four even throws, eight spaces; five even throws, 16 spaces (the limit of bonus moves for the Phantom is 16 spaces). As soon as an odd number is thrown, no more bonus moves are added on. The Phantom is moved ahead, and his turn is over. The first "player" to go around the track wins the game. (If the *player* lands on a star, he plays the standard version of the "Bonus moves letter game.")

VARIATION

Heads and Tails Auto Race

Suggested age 9 and up

Time 20 to 35 minutes

Object To be the first driver to complete a lap around the track

Materials Bag of commercial letter tiles or letter slips, game path in one player's notebook, felt pen or crayon for each player, spinner (numbered 1 to 6), penny in a glass jar, watch with second hand or one-minute egg timer

Preparation Draw the game path for Double or Nothing Auto Race but write "Flip" in the spaces where it says "Out of gas" or "Full speed ahead."

If you are using commercial letter tiles, remove the J, Q, U, V, X, and Z. If not, tear up 20 slips of paper and write one letter of the alphabet on each, omitting the above-mentioned letters. Put all the slips into a paper bag.

Put a penny in a glass jar and replace the lid.

Rules The first player spins the spinner and, beginning at Start, moves along the game path the indicated number of spaces by writing his first initial in each box he passes through. If he lands on a spot that says "Flip," he must shake the jar with the coin. If heads comes up, he may take an extra turn, but if tails comes up, he loses his next turn. Whenever he lands on a star, he gets to play the Heads and Tails Game. To play, he picks two letter tiles or slips from the bag—let's say D and W. He calls out one of these letters, perhaps D, and then shakes the coin in the jar to see if D will be the "head" of the word (the first letter) or the "tail" of the word (the last letter). Naturally, the W will be put in the other position. Now the player has one minute to call out words with the designated first and last letters. For example, if W was heads (and D tails), the player may say "wood," "word," "wand," "weed," and so on. At the end of one minute, the player may move forward one space for each correct word. (Proper nouns, slang, and abbreviations are not permitted.) If he picks two of the *same* letter (as may happen with commercial letter tiles), the words the player supplies must begin and end with that letter. Letters should always be returned to the bag after the player's turn.

If a player lands on the shortcut space by exact count, he may take the shorter route. The first player to reach or cross the finish line wins the game (exact count is not necessary).

Happy Holiday!

Suggested age   5 and up

Time   15 to 35 minutes

Object   To be the first player to collect all the letters in the word "holiday"

Materials   Game path and felt pen for each player, one die or spinner, paper bag with "holiday" slips, watch with second hand or one-minute egg timer

Preparation   Draw the game path shown into each player's notebook. There should be eight boxes on each side of the square, the letters in the word "holiday" as shown, four suns, and three rain clouds.

Pull a sheet out of your spiral notebook and tear it into 12 slips. On seven of them, write the letters H, O, L, I, D, A, and Y. Leave the other five blank and put all 12 slips into a paper bag.

Rules   The first player shoots the die and, beginning at start, moves the number of squares indicated by drawing a diagonal line in each box he passes through. If he lands in a blank space, his turn is over, and the next player goes. If he lands on a letter, he has the chance to win it. To do so, he has one minute to make any of the players in the car *laugh*. He can make funny faces, noises or motions, but he can't tickle or touch the other players. The others must watch the person who is trying to make them laugh and must keep their hands at their sides. If the player is successful, he wins the letter he landed on and writes it on the bottom of his notebook page (if not, nothing happens). If a player lands on a sun, he may pick a slip from the bag. If he picks one with a letter he doesn't have yet, he wins that letter and may write it at the bottom of his page. (If he picks a letter he already has or a blank slip, nothing happens.) In any case, he returns the slip to the bag when his turn is over. Any time the player lands on a rain cloud, he also picks a slip. If he picks a letter that he already has, he must cross it off his list. However, if it's a letter he doesn't have or a blank slip, nothing happens.

Players keep going around the path trying to earn or win the letters they need to spell the word "holiday." The second time around the path, they draw a second diagonal line in each box to complete the letter X. The third time around they draw a vertical line, and the fourth time they draw a horizontal line. Of course, it's unlikely that it will take that long for any one player to collect the letters to spell "holiday." The game stops as soon as one player has collected all the necessary letters. However, if no one has collected all the letters needed after four times around the board, the player who has collected the most letters wins the game.

Adaptation for one player Use the same game path as for the standard version. If the player lands on a letter, he has one minute to write down as many words as he can that begin with that letter (a younger child can say them out loud). Score one point for each word. Then he shoots a pair of dice. If his total score for the word game is *higher* than the amount shown on the dice, he wins the letter. However, if it's the same or less, nothing happens. If he lands on a sun or rain cloud, he picks a slip as in the standard version.

The player may go around the board three times. If he still hasn't collected all the letters he needs after three times around the path, he loses the game. If he can do it after two times around, he's a champ!

You Dirty Dog!

Suggested age 6 and up

Time 15 to 30 minutes

Object To get the highest "clean score" by the time you reach the end of the game path or, at least, the lowest "dirty score"

Materials Different color felt pen for each player, one game path, standard spinner, numbered 1 to 6

Preparation Copy the game path into one player's notebook. Make 37 spaces on the path including the start and finish boxes.

You Dirty Dog!

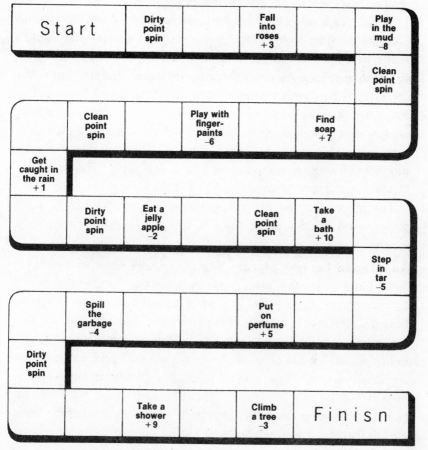

Rules Each player should make two columns on a separate page of his notebook—one to record "clean" scores (plus scores) and one to record "dirty" scores (minus scores).

The first player spins the spinner and, beginning in the start box, moves along his game path the indicated amount of spaces by drawing a vertical line of his color in each box that he passes through. If a player lands on a blank space, he does nothing, and the next player goes. If he lands on a square which tells him to record a plus score or minus score, he writes the score in the appropriate column. Whenever a player lands on a square that says "Dirty point spin" or "Clean point spin," he spins the spinner again and *doubles* the number that the arrow points to. For example, if the spinner lands on 4, he doubles it to make 8. If he is spinning for "clean" points, he adds that number to his plus column. If he is spinning for "dirty" points, he adds that number to his minus column. Players take turns and continue along the board from start to finish (exact count is *not* necessary). It doesn't matter who finishes first. All players get to complete the entire path. When everyone is finished, players add all the scores in their *plus* columns (the "clean" scores) and all the scores in their *minus* columns (the "dirty" scores). The total minus score is subtracted from the total plus score for a final total. This may be a positive or negative number.

The player with the highest positive score wins the game. If no player has a positive score, the one with the *lowest* negative score wins the game.

Adaptation for one player The player uses one game path for himself and a Phantom player. He moves along the path for himself by drawing one diagonal line with a red felt pen in each box he passes through. He moves for the Phantom by drawing one diagonal line with a blue or black felt pen in each box the Phantom passes through. Both "players" move along the game path in the same way as in the standard version. The player keeps a separate score sheet for himself and for the Phantom. When the player and the Phantom have both traveled along the entire path, scores are totaled the same way as they are in the standard game. The "player" with the highest plus score or lowest minus score wins the game.

Making Board Games

You can make your family's favorite car games into more permanent board games to use again and again in the car and at home. Here are a few ways to make durable game boards.

Rectangular paths with sliding movers Some of the board games in this book already have rectangular paths which are easy to transfer onto oak tag (poster board). Others have winding paths which can be converted into rectangular ones. To do so, simply count the number of boxes on the winding path and put the same number on the rectangular path (see the illustration).

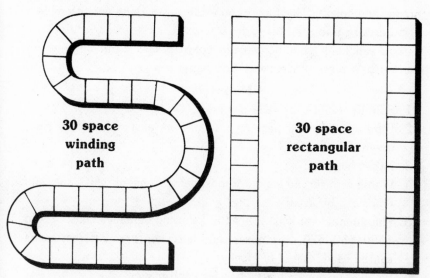

30 space
winding
path

30 space
rectangular
path

Use an 11 × 14 sheet of oak tag, and draw the rectangular path right along the borders of the oak tag. As movers you can use bobby pins of different shades and/or paper clips, colored with different felt-tip pens. To move around the board, simply slip the bobby pin or paper clip onto the board and slide it forward or backward along the path.

Paths of any shape with peg movers Draw the game path on an 11" × 14" sheet of oak tag, making each box along the path as large as possible. Before writing any information in the boxes, poke two or three holes at the bottom of each one with a sharp object, such as the point of a compass. As movers, you can use different colored pegs from a set, or paper fasteners with the heads colored in.

Boards to use at home All of the games in this book can be played at home except for the highway observation games in Chapter

2. If you're making a game board which will be used under stationary conditions, you don't have to make special clip-on or peg movers. You can draw your boards on a large piece of heavy cardboard (such as the side of a carton) or draw it on white oak tag pasted onto the cardboard. As movers, you can use playing pieces from a commercial game, different coins, poker chips, or any small objects you find around the house. This type of board is durable and will resemble a commercial game.

You can keep your homemade board games clean by covering them with a piece of clear Con-tact paper.

Materials

1. Spiral notebook for each player
2. Different color felt pens or crayons—at least red, yellow, blue, green, and brown
3. Paper bag
4. Watch with second hand (for most games, one- or two-minute egg timer can be used)
5. Play money—at least 20 of the following denominations: $500, $100, $50, $20, $10 (poker chips in two or three different colors can be used instead of money)
6. Small envelope or plastic bag for each player
7. Pair of dice in clear glass jar (standard spinner or deck of playing cards can usually be used instead of dice)
8. Standard deck of playing cards held together with rubber band
9. Magnetic checker set
10. Travel edition of the SCRABBLE® Crossword Game

Optional Materials

1. Commercial letter tiles

Afterword

A car can be more than a mode of transportation. It can also be a vehicle of discovery—a vehicle devoid of the usual household interruptions, a place which offers time not already accounted for.

Use my games as springboards for creating entirely new ones! Use my storytelling ideas as passageways to story ideas of your own! Enjoy the "trip" of growing with your children and sharing the pleasures of their childhood. It's a trip that is all too short.

Wishing you joy in all your travels,

Sandy Beram

Harvey Beram

Glen Beram

Age Index

Since the interests and skills of children vary, this is merely a rough guide for the ages necessary for playing the games in this book. Older children and adults will enjoy all the games, even those for the youngest ages. You can check off the games you've played (and mark your favorites) in the boxes on the left.

CATEGORY INDEX